"By highlighting the career of Geoffrey Fisher against the background of the dramatic times and cultural changes through which he lived, David Hein offers a judicious and insightful portrait. Fisher's accomplishments and shortcomings stand out in this lucid biography."

—Bishop Frederick Borsch
Lutheran Theological Seminary at Philadelphia

"David Hein's treatment of Archbishop Fisher's career throws a great deal of light on the Church of England, Britain in the mid-twentieth century, and the place of religion in Europe and in the developing world following World War II. His assessment of Fisher as leader of the international Anglican Communion is particularly illuminating."

—W. Brown Patterson
Emeritus, University of the South

"This short, accessible book is helpful to both the professional scholar and interested amateur who wish to gain a greater understanding of the Church of England and the Anglican Communion more widely during the turbulent post-war period."

—Wendy Dackson
Ripon College, Cuddesdon

Geoffrey Fisher

Princeton Theological Monograph Series

K. C. Hanson and Charles M. Collier, Series Editors

Recent volumes in the series

Bonnie L. Pattison
Poverty in the Theology of John Calvin

Anette Ejsing
A Theology of Anticipation: A Constructive Study of C. S. Peirce

Michael G. Cartwright
*Practices, Politics, and Performance:
Toward a Communal Hermeneutic for Christian Ethics*

Stephen Finlan and Vladimir Kharlamov, editors
Theōsis: Deification in Christian Theology

John A. Vissers
The Neo-Orthodox Theology of W. W. Bryden

Sam Hamstra, editor
The Reformed Pastor by John Williamson Nevin

Byron C. Bangert
*Consenting to God and Nature:
Toward a Theocentric, Naturalistic, Theological Ethics*

Richard Valantasis et al., editors
*The Subjective Eye:
Essays in Honor of Margaret Miles*

Caryn Riswold
*Coram Deo:
Human Life in the Vision of God*

Paul O. Ingram, editor
Constructing a Relational Cosmology

T. David Beck
The Holy Spirit and the Renewal of All Things

Geoffrey Fisher

Archbishop of Canterbury, 1945–1961

David Hein

Pickwick *Publications*

An imprint of *Wipf and Stock Publishers*
199 West 8th Avenue • Eugene OR 97401

GEOFFREY FISHER
Archbishop of Canterbury, 1945–1961

Princeton Theological Monograph Series 77

ISBN 13: 978-1-59752-824-5

Cataloging-in-Publication data

Hein, David
Geoffrey Fisher : archbishop of Canterbury, 1945–1961 / David Hein.

    Eugene, OR: Pickwick Publications 2008
    Princeton Theological Monograph Series 77
        xviii + 122 p. ; 23 cm.
        Includes bibliographical references.

    ISBN 13: 978-1-59752-824-5 (alk. paper)

    1. Fisher of Lambeth, Geoffrey Francis Fisher, Baron, 1887–1972.
2. Church of England—Bishops—Biography. 3. Anglican Communion—Bishops—Biography. I. Title. II. Series.

    BX5199.F57 H45 2007

Cover photograph of Geoffrey Fisher © 1960 Lewis Morley Archive / National Portrait Gallery, London

Manufactured in the U.S.A.

To my nephew, Charlie

Contents

Abbreviations / x

Introduction / xi

1 Formation: 1887–1932 / 1

2 Chester and London: 1932–1945 / 17

3 Archbishop of Canterbury, 1945–1961:
  The Church of England / 37

4 Archbishop of Canterbury, 1945–1961:
  The Anglican Communion / 57

5 Archbishop of Canterbury, 1945–1961:
  Ecumenical Outreach / 71

6 Archbishop of Canterbury, 1945–1961:
  Church and State / 83

7 Retirement: 1961–1972 / 99

Bibliography / 115

Abbreviations

CGL Papers	Cosmo Gordon Lang Papers, Lambeth Palace Library, London
DNB	*Dictionary of National Biography*
GF	Geoffrey Fisher
GF Papers	Geoffrey Fisher Papers, Lambeth Palace Library
LPL	Lambeth Palace Library
ODCC	*Oxford Dictionary of the Christian Church*
SPCK	Society for Promoting Christian Knowledge

Introduction

THE ninety-eighth Primate of All England, William Temple, died in 1944, and the following year Winston Churchill named Geoffrey Fisher as his successor in the Chair of St. Augustine of Canterbury. The prime minister's choice proved controversial, however, because another man, Bishop George Bell of Chichester, looked to many the wiser appointment. What was indisputable was the severity of the challenges that the new archbishop would face. The Second World War would soon be over, and then the mammoth project of rebuilding would commence in earnest. For both the church and the nation, this effort of reconstruction would be spiritual as well as material.

Out of the Ruins

Few if any historians could evoke the postwar mood or depict the moral and physical ruins of civilization as effectively as the English novelist Rose Macaulay in her 1950 novel, *The World My Wilderness*, set in the years just following World War II.[1] In this book the author expresses in a clear and moving way her fears about the future of British society. This novel, she said, "is about the ruins of the City [the business center of London], and the general wreckage of the world that they seem to stand for. And about a rather lost and strayed and derelict girl who made them her spiritual home."[2]

Although only seventeen (and the daughter of a King's Counsel), this central figure, Barbary, is already barbarous: wild, intractable, given to acts of defiance and petty theft. "'Civilised . . .' Barbary seemed to examine civilisation, balancing it gravely, perhaps wistfully, against something else, and to reject it, as if it were mentioned too late" (33). The child of a broken home, during the war she had lived in the South of France with her beautiful, intelligent, idle, pleasure-loving mother, whose notion of parental love did not entail a heavy investment in adult supervision.

1. Macaulay, *The World My Wilderness;* hereinafter cited within the text.
2. Macaulay, *Letters to a Friend, 1950–1952*, 27.

As a member of a band of boys and girls assisting the Maquis during the Occupation, Barbary was brutally and far too rapidly transformed from a child of innocence into a child of experience. After the war, living in London, she remains somewhat of an anarchist, preferring to live amid "the ruined waste lands . . . the broken walls and foundations . . . the roofless, gaping churches, the stone flights of stairs climbing high into emptiness" (61). These places, she feels, are where she belongs: at "the waste margins of civilisation . . . , where other outcasts lurked, and questions were not asked" (110).

In this novel, Rose Macaulay is shining the light of her torch on the spiritual wreckage of postwar Britain—on the desolate areas of both cities and souls that leaders such as Geoffrey Fisher would have to search out and tend to. In a violent and treacherous world, one that bears a growing resemblance to a moral wasteland, Macaulay is asking: How many Barbarys might we be producing? How many children may be growing up too fast, lacking adequate care and security, and hence rootless, sullen, suspicious, and defiant? This novel is full of compassion toward all of its characters, but especially toward Barbary, who, as one literary scholar wrote in summarizing the author's attitude toward her creation, "is thoroughly lost, thoroughly pathetic, and very much worth saving."[3]

Toward the end of *The World My Wilderness*, Macaulay appears to raise a final question: Does the church have a role to play in this work of rebuilding? While Barbary's only religious belief is "in hell" (174), her half-brother Richie—who fought in the war, endured three years in a German POW camp, escaped, and now desires only the beauty and refinement of "aristocratic culture" (150)—is drawn to the church. But the lure appears to be largely aesthetic and nostalgic: "In this pursuit he was impelled sometimes beyond his reasoning self, to grasp at the rich . . . panoplies, the swinging censors, of churches from whose creeds and uses he was alien, because at least they embodied some continuance, some tradition" (150).

In the last pages of the novel, however, Richie literally takes steps toward the church, possibly reflecting a deeper quest for order and meaning in his life and in the lives of others. Fully conscious of the barbarian threat ("the primeval chaos and old night"), he murmurs to himself T. S. Eliot's words from *The Wasteland*: "We are in rats' alleys, where the dead men lost their bones" (253). Then, "[s]huddering a little, he took the track across the wilderness and towards St. Paul's [Cathedral]. Behind him, the questionable chaos of broken courts and inns lay sprawled under

---

3. Webster, *After the Trauma*, 27.

the October mist, and the shells of churches gaped like lost myths, and the jungle pressed in on them, seeking to cover them up" (253–54).

What the church received with the appointment of Geoffrey Fisher to the see of Canterbury was, at the very least, a man of strength, discipline, and tenacity—indeed, a former headmaster—who would not readily submit to either primeval or ecclesiastical chaos. Everything that he did was connected to the service of one overriding goal: building up the church, and thereby enlarging the clearing in the wilderness.

A Pivotal Archiepiscopate

Overshadowed both by his famous predecessor, the philosopher and ecumenist William Temple, and by his widely loved successor, the theologian and spiritual guide Michael Ramsey, Geoffrey Francis Fisher (1887–1972), ninety-ninth archbishop of Canterbury, has largely been ignored by professional historians. But in fact his was a pivotal archiepiscopate, one that cries out for fresh examination. The problems and initiatives of his tenure anticipated the major events in Anglican church history and theology in the decades that followed.

Fisher's period in office began and ended with the bridge-building work of ecumenism. Preaching at Cambridge in 1946, he urged the Church of England and the Free Churches to work toward establishing "full communion": sharing the sacraments with one another but stopping short of complete union. And in 1960, at the end of his tenure in office, Fisher embarked on a tour that included stops in Jerusalem, Istanbul, and Rome. His meeting with Pope John XXIII marked the first time that an archbishop of Canterbury had visited the Holy See since Archbishop Thomas Arundel undertook the journey in 1397.

Fisher was also the key person in building up the modern Anglican Communion. In the 1950s his trips to West Africa, Central Africa, and East Africa were major parts of his successful effort to establish new provinces within the Communion. Indeed, his work anticipated the transformation of the British Empire from a far-flung imperial domain into a commonwealth of equal states. His frequent visits to Canada and the United States, coupled with his efforts to include the American bishops and others in the deliberations of the Lambeth Conference, helped to make the Anglican Communion an experienced reality for many Anglicans and Episcopalians outside Britain.

Of particular interest, too, is the relationship between the Church of England and the nation. The senior prelate whom millions of people around the world watched as he conducted the coronation ceremony for Queen Elizabeth II in June 1953, Fisher has been referred to as the last great Establishment archbishop of Canterbury. After him, British society and the churches were forced to change, responding to increased immigration, religious pluralism, and secularization. Worthy of attention are such subjects as Fisher's intervention in the Suez Crisis, his involvement in debates on the use of atomic weapons, and his understanding of the role of the Church of England within the larger society. It is important to discern the positive as well as the negative aspects of establishment. A key to Fisher might well be his strong sense of the pervasive responsibility of the Established Church within English society. This commitment influenced not only his responses (sometimes supportive, often critical) to government initiatives but also his understanding of the place of the Church of England in relation to the other churches.

Fisher's time in London, first as bishop of London (1939–45) and then as archbishop of Canterbury, was a period of war, devastation, and rebuilding in the capital city and the nation. How well did Fisher prepare the Church of England for what followed? What were the strengths and weaknesses of his approach to the task of fortifying the church—and the Anglican Communion—for the future? What were his personal strengths and weaknesses as a leader for this crucial time in the history of Christian institutions?

This Fisher-shaped time of both reconstruction and fresh initiatives was a bridge period for the church. One aspect of his work that should attract our attention is not only what an archbishop of Canterbury can do during such a time but also what he chooses not to do. The Cambridge theologian Donald MacKinnon was one of those who regretted that George Bell, bishop of Chichester, did not succeed Temple at Canterbury in 1944–45. Certainly Fisher lacked Bell's adventurous spirit, but it is interesting to see what an administrator of Fisher's ability is able to accomplish. Part of that work undoubtedly has to do with working hard to bring about conditions within which other men and women, who possess different gifts, can flourish.

This biography is intended to be a thought-provoking examination of an important figure in a transitional era. At the same time, this book will offer a balanced portrait: Fisher's tendency as archbishop to play the rule-oriented headmaster, his emphasis on administration rather than on theology and spirituality, and his lack of personal charisma undercut his long-term impact. A fresh review of Fisher's virtues and deficiencies as an ecclesiastical statesman is needed.

Geoffrey Fisher's tenure represents a distinctive approach to the office. His was not only a particularly significant archiepiscopate, one in which the central issues of his time and place are reflected. It was also a tenure that emphasized the archbishop as chief executive of a large and complex organization. Fisher personified one major way of inhabiting his role: the archbishop as administrator.

Through his example, then, we can gain some perspective on both the positive and the negative features of this archiepiscopal modus operandi, both in his own day and for succeeding generations. Being a highly competent administrator means more than being an efficient manager. It requires thoughtful strategic planning as well as day-to-day administration. But this style of leadership may result in a loss of personal stature, influence, and memorability if the archbishop's focus is largely on structure rather than on qualities of mind and spirit: if, in other words, the archbishop is not also known—and effective—as an intellectual force, a social prophet, or a wise spiritual teacher. The subject of this biography does suggest an irony: Geoffrey Fisher may well have been a more competent archbishop than either his successor or his predecessor, but somehow they are the ones whom later generations are more likely to remember.

The Plan of This Book

Unlike the two earlier, book-length treatments of Fisher's life and career, this biography is much shorter. Especially compared with Edward Carpenter's massive, 800-page account, the present work more closely resembles a sketch of the life or simply a long introduction. It is more likely to give the reader a sense of the forest than a detailed acquaintance with all the flora and fauna. For that reason, however, this narrative may be more useful to beginning researchers and more accessible to anyone seeking an overview of the principal contours of this archbishop's life-story. Further details may be found not only in Carpenter's *Archbishop Fisher* but also in the specialized journal literature and in the 400 boxes of Fisher Papers in the Lambeth Palace Library, in London.

This book consists of seven brief chapters:

Chapter 1, "Formation: 1887–1932," discusses Fisher's family background, education, early career as a schoolmaster, and his long tenure as headmaster of Repton (where he succeeded William Temple in 1914). This chapter looks at the influence of his family and upbringing, and it focuses on Fisher's years as headmaster, an experience that undoubtedly shaped his approach to episcopal office.

Chapter 2, "Chester and London: 1932–1945," begins with Fisher's service as bishop of Chester and then takes up his tenure in a key post in the Church of England. In 1939 he became bishop of London, bringing effective oversight to a diocese that had been poorly administered for many years. This chapter offers a look at Fisher's role as the head of a committee for pastoral reorganization necessitated by war damage, at his work as chairman of the Archbishops' War Committee, at his effort to impose some ecclesiastical order in his diocese by issuing regulations on ritual conformity, and at his ecumenical participation with Roman Catholics in the Sword of the Spirit movement.

The heart of this book, chapters 3 through 6, provides an account of Fisher's tenure as the spiritual head of the Anglican Communion. His tenure of office comprised the crucial years from the end of the Second World War to the beginning of the 1960s. For these four chapters taken as a whole, the principle of organization is both topical and topographical, for these chapters are presented in the order of widening concentric circles of archiepiscopal activity: the Church of England, the Anglican Communion, other Christian communions, and the world beyond the church.

Chapter 3, "Archbishop of Canterbury, 1945–1961: The Church of England," begins with the story of Fisher's selection by Prime Minister Winston Churchill to succeed William Temple as archbishop of Canterbury. This chapter examines Fisher's attention to canon-law revision, his response to the controversial case of Bishop Barnes and his book *The Rise of Christianity*, and his establishment of the Church Commissioners.

Chapter 4, "Archbishop of Canterbury, 1945–1961: The Anglican Communion," reviews Fisher's activity on behalf of the worldwide Anglican Communion. The 99th archbishop of Canterbury worked hard to strengthen ties with American Episcopalians, and he successfully led two Lambeth Conferences (1948 and 1958). His efforts to establish autonomous provinces in Africa had particularly important results. This chapter briefly discusses Fisher's appointment of Bishop Stephen F. Bayne as executive officer of the Anglican Communion.

Chapter 5, "Archbishop of Canterbury, 1945–1961: Ecumenical Outreach," considers Fisher's vigorous labors on behalf of Christian unity. It describes the ecumenical efforts made during his archiepiscopate, beginning with his Cambridge sermon on reunion. It then discusses Fisher's involvement with the World Council of Churches, which he served as chairman at its inauguration in 1948. This chapter concludes with Fisher's historic trip to Jerusalem, Istanbul, and Rome.

Chapter 6, "Archbishop of Canterbury, 1945–1961: Church and State," begins with a discussion of ecclesiastical establishment. It then examines Fisher's involvement in debates concerning premium bonds, the Suez Crisis, and nuclear weapons. A look at Fisher's participation in the coronation of Queen Elizabeth II rounds off the chapter.

Chapter 7, "Retirement: 1961–1972," sketches Fisher's activities in retirement as a curate in the village of Trent in Dorset and as an active participant in the debate over Anglican-Methodist reunion. This chapter includes a discussion of leadership and ends with an assessment of Fisher's strengths and weaknesses.

Facing the Future

For most people in the United Kingdom, life at the end of the Fisher era at Lambeth looked very different from the way it did at the inception of his archiepiscopate. Probably to many outside observers the Church of England did not seem to change very much in the traditionalist 1950s, but no one could fail to remark that society as a whole was undergoing a significant transformation. In financial terms alone, the British people by 1961 were significantly better off than they had been in 1946, and they had reason to hope for continued gains. Greater purchasing power brought with it widespread access to labor-saving appliances as well as to automobiles and television sets. It was the beginning of a new, more prosperous era, with fewer restrictions and more freedom in all areas of life. But it was also an age that generated a fresh wave of anxieties about meaning, order, and security.

Published in 1950, Rose Macaulay's *The World My Wilderness* is very much a postwar novel. Published only six years later, her last book, *The Towers of Trebizond*, already anticipates the mood of the 1960s. Despite the seriousness of its leading themes, this later novel has a much jauntier tone than the earlier work, which is unremittingly bleak. And *Trebizond* presents the religious questions even more squarely. Indeed, its main subject is the relation of faith and doubt in this exciting but rather frightening new era, when new possibilities were beginning to open up and old patterns of life were breaking apart. The central character in the novel is a young woman named Laurie, who likens the Church of England to "a great empire on its way out, that holds its subjects by poetic force. . . . [T]hough for ever reeling, the towers [representing the church] do not fall . . . ."[4]

4. Macaulay, *The Towers of Trebizond*, 234. See Hein, "Faith and Doubt in Rose

Upon leaving office and going into retirement, Geoffrey Fisher did not see the church as being "on its way out." He said, "I leave the Church of England in good heart."[5] But the historian and theologian Adrian Hastings raises an intriguing point when he observes that several women writers of this period—not only Rose Macaulay but also Barbara Pym (in *A Glass of Blessings*), Iris Murdoch (in *The Bell*), and Pamela Hansford Johnson (in *The Humbler Creation*)—were producing novels with a different (and more accurate?) take on contemporary Anglican life and the future of the Church of England.

The 1950s, Hastings writes, were a "rather Anglican decade, and Anglican of a benignly conservative hue." That's the Fisher era, reflected in each of these novels, where "the Church appears on the surface as a relatively prospering institution with a decidedly traditionalist orientation."[6] But in the view of all four of these novelists, "A Church apparently very much in business turns out in each case to be . . . worm-eaten. . . . [T]he impression given is one of a nice, rather ineffectual, socially respectable but bewildered rump not far off its last legs."[7]

Hastings intimates little by way of appraisal of these writers' impressions. At this point in his narrative, his contribution to ecclesiastical history is neither to endorse nor to oppose their views but simply to ferret out and to highlight these fictional accounts, giving his readers the opportunity to consider what truth might be contained therein. Within the limited terms of the present study, we might keep these novels in mind when we evaluate Geoffrey Fisher's record as archbishop of Canterbury.

Acknowledgments

Special thanks to the Historical Society of the Episcopal Church for a research grant in support of this project and to the staff of the Lambeth Palace Library for their expert assistance with all aspects of the life and career of Geoffrey Fisher.

Macaulay's *The Towers of Trebizond*."

    5. Quoted in Hastings, *A History of English Christianity, 1920–2000*, 452.

    6. Ibid., 451–52.

    7. Ibid., 452.

1

Formation: 1887–1932

GEOFFREY Francis Fisher was, by and large, an uncomplicated man. Neither enticed by rebellion nor drawn by doubt, he was conservative and consistent, a loyal and devoted churchman. His considerable powers, both intellectual and physical, were steadily and happily employed in the service of established institutions.

Self-aware without being self-absorbed, he would have recognized the applicability to his own case of the Romantic poet William Wordsworth's famous dictum that "The Child is father of the Man." Fisher would have appreciated the suitability of these words as an evocation of the trajectory of his life from birth: the clerical forebears, the village rectory, the parish church, the intelligent and contented child, the purposeful young clergyman—and then steady advancement, largely unsought. Prepared over generations and seasoned beyond his years, Fisher already possessed, at age twenty-seven, sufficient gravitas to convince others that he had the necessary equipment to rule with authority. Years later, as archbishop of Canterbury, he remained, observers noted, very much the headmaster: a good, effective head, but still the law-giving administrator.

A consistency of character and outlook marks his life, then, just as a certain consistency or conservatism marks this era in the history of the Church of England—and especially the Fisher years at Lambeth—before the tumultuous 1960s. Thus the first chapter of this book, perhaps to an unusual degree for a biographical study, delineates the contours of what follows in succeeding chapters. In a sense, there are no surprises after this first chapter, for all that Fisher did was rooted in the core convictions that he acquired in his formative years.

At the same time, however, a career path is not a cross-country course; the vagaries of even a conservative human nature and the play of chance wreak havoc with predictions. In the case of Geoffrey Fisher, intelligence and initiative, yoked with determination and drive, were essential ingredients of his make-up, developments of the personal and social capital acquired during his youth. At the start of his public career, therefore, no one could say for certain either what challenges time and circumstance would confront him with or what use he would make of the opportunities that providence or fortune set before him. But the early years provide strong clues.

Higham-on-the-Hill, Leicestershire

A remarkable consistency marks Geoffrey Fisher's family background. In 1772 his great-grandfather, a clergyman by the name of John Fisher, was appointed to the benefice (an endowed church office providing a living) of Higham-on-the-Hill. Three miles from the market town of Nuneaton, Higham was then a small agricultural village of some three or four hundred people in Leicestershire, a county in central England that lies east of Birmingham and northeast of Coventry. He held this benefice until his death sixty years later. As the living was in the gift of the family, it could be handed down from one generation to the next. Eventually John Fisher's son and his grandson—as well as his great-grandson, Legh, one of Geoffrey's elder brothers—would hold the same position, ministering to this small community in the Midlands.[1] In the temporal lot he drew, Geoffrey Fisher's father, Henry, who served the church of Higham-on-the-Hill for more than forty years, was perhaps the most fortunate, because, as Edward Carpenter has observed, "the rise in status of the rural parson [reached] its peak in the eighties when the rectory often became the centre of a revived village life."[2]

Geoffrey Fisher was born at Higham on May 5, 1887, the youngest of ten children. His mother, Katherine Richmond Fisher, he later recalled, was "a very lovely, very handsome woman with a great presence."[3] With her, Geoffrey enjoyed a special bond. She had a good sense of humor, enjoyed playing games with her children, and ran the rectory effectively, becoming its emotional center.[4] Her youngest child called her "the presiding genius" of his childhood home, "a great stronghold in the whole life of the house."[5]

---

1. Palmer, *A Class of Their Own*, 153.
2. Carpenter, *Archbishop Fisher*, 4.
3. Quoted in Purcell, *Fisher of Lambeth*, 30.
4. Carpenter, *Archbishop Fisher*, 5.
5. Quoted in ibid.

Born at Higham-on-the-Hill in 1837 and educated at Jesus College, Cambridge University, Geoffrey's father in middle age was a spare, shy, industrious man. On behalf of the denizens of both the village and the countryside, he was comfortable and conscientious in carrying out his duties. As a preacher, however, he tended to be long-winded and uninspiring, except on those occasions when he became too excited and worked up in the pulpit.[6]

Undoubtedly, his parishioners, like sermon auditors everywhere, would have preferred to listen to better preaching. But it is important to remember that the Anglicanism of the Victorian rural village was a distinctive form of Christianity, whose center was not necessarily the Sunday-morning sermon. This form of Christianity was a far cry, for example, from today's neo-evangelical megachurch, for whom the minister is, first and foremost, an engaging preacher: everything in that style of worship leads up to and follows from the proclamation of the message. Although he may have been more Protestant than Catholic in his Anglican sensibilities, Geoffrey Fisher never viewed the role of the clergyman in such restrictive terms. In his father's practice in the environs of Higham, Geoffrey would have seen the priest as a minister who spreads the evangel by living a particular kind of life within the community. Ideally, the clergyman would instantiate in his own person the truths of his faith and the virtues of daily living, teaching by example as much as by precept.

This approach to ministry was part of a characteristically Anglican understanding of the duties of a priest. It stressed personal engagement, pastoral care, and prayer: the clergyman as mediator and exemplar.[7] An Anglican priest could best be depicted, then, not primarily as a preacher but as a *parson*, whose value depended upon the quality of his person. As the eighteenth-century legal scholar William Blackstone wrote in his famous *Commentaries*, a priest "is called parson, *persona*, because by his person the church, which is an invisible body, is represented."[8]

Typically in this era the parish church was the center of the community, and this was the case at Higham.[9] As A. N. Wilson notes, the local church was the "place where communities gathered—partly for worship, partly for music, ribaldry, and gossip, partly for nebulous reasons which did not need to be defined"; and this habitual use of the church went on

6. Ibid.

7. Hein, *Noble Powell and the Episcopal Establishment in the Twentieth Century,* 4.

8. Blackstone, *Commentaries on the Laws of England,* 1:372.

9. "[T]he parish church of Higham on the Hill and its local school exercised an influence which the two Methodist chapels could not rival." Carpenter, *Archbishop Fisher,* 344.

long "after the box pews were removed."[10] Of course, far too often the village parson did not match the ideal but instead was ill trained, indolent, focused more on cricket than on theology, and therefore roundly ineffectual. In many instances if parishioners went to church for a religious reason it was not to hear good preaching but rather, as Adrian Hastings says, "to draw some spark of inspiration from the Cranmerian vocabulary of a sung matins, from pillars and vaults and monuments, but seldom from the clergy."[11]

In fine, the Fishers were a family well integrated into this little community of Higham-on-the-Hill, which was, as Geoffrey Fisher later said, "the background and the life-blood of everything."[12] That is, the quality of community itself—what the Germans call *Gemeinschaft*—was the vital element that coursed through the overlapping social spheres in which young Fisher found himself. As sources of meaning and identity, these circles of association were formative of the future archbishop. To use his phrases, there were "the community and my family in the rectory," "the community of the village and all its doings," and "the community of the church in which all of us had our place."[13]

Throughout his life and professional career, Geoffrey Fisher would find fulfillment—and seek fulfillment for others—in appropriate structures. Like a good Burkean, he carried deep in his bones the belief that order is the only environment within which true freedom can thrive and human beings can flourish. By both nature and nurture, he was bred to believe in arrangements in which everyone could find his or her place.

Education

After a brief stay in the Higham village school, Geoffrey—age eight—went to Lindley Lodge, a local preparatory school of forty boys. Located within walking distance of the rectory, this school was his academic home for six years. His record during his first term was poor, but he worked hard to shore up areas in which he was initially weak. He eventually rose to the top of the school in Latin, Greek, French, English, and mathematics. At Lindley Lodge, he received a good preparatory education, he learned how

10. Wilson, *After the Victorians*, 305.

11. Hastings, *A History of English Christianity, 1920–2000*, 71.

12. Quoted in Purcell, *Fisher of Lambeth*, 29.

13. Quoted in Carpenter, *Archbishop Fisher*, 7.

to take responsibility for boys placed in his charge, and he worked hard at sports even when he had little natural aptitude for them.[14]

In September 1901, at the age of 14, Geoffrey entered Marlborough College, in Wiltshire (a county in southern England), on a foundation scholarship. Established to provide an education for the sons of clergymen, this public school opened in 1843. Here Geoffrey Fisher excelled—as scholar, as student leader (he made a brave and resolute senior prefect), and even as young Christian. He apparently never experienced a spiritual crisis; the religion of his youth and young adulthood was in important respects continuous with the faith in which he was raised. "I learned," he later said of these years, "how to tackle everything that came along in what I now recognize was an intelligent Christian way, not borrowing from Christ, but translating into my daily duties and occupations and pleasures the spirit which flowed from His revelation of the Kingdom of God."[15]

From Marlborough, Geoffrey went up to Oxford on a scholarship in October 1906. His college, Exeter, was founded in 1314 by Walter de Stapeldon, bishop of Exeter (who, 12 years later, was murdered by a London mob). By Geoffrey Fisher's time, Exeter College had 182 students and eight Fellows. Anglican tradition still predominated there. The rector of Exeter College was a priest, W. W. Jackson, and students were required to attend one Sunday service in the chapel and four weekday services.[16]

Fisher acquitted himself well at Oxford, becoming president of the junior common room, a fine athlete (he was captain of his college boat club and was given his colors for rugby), and an outstanding student. He went down with a triple first, having gained first-class honours in Mods (Classical Moderations: Greek and Latin literature) in 1908, in Greats (*Literae Humaniores*: philosophy and ancient history) in 1910, and in theology in 1911. Fisher always had a good, clear head, but he seems never to have had a particularly adventurous or curious mind—which is itself rather curious in someone so bright.[17] He was simply not attracted by intellectual questions, such as current debates in biblical criticism, or prone to challenge received opinion, at least past a certain point. He had, one might say, the right sort of intelligence for the practical problems of administration. He would not have made a first-rate scholar, however, for

14. Ibid., 6–7.
15. Quoted in ibid., 10.
16. Ibid., 11.
17. Ibid., 12.

scholars must be intellectually imaginative and also persistently dissatis-fied, even skeptical, in a way that Fisher never was.

But Geoffrey Fisher did have an imagination for friendship. While at Oxford he became a good friend of the eccentric Anglo-Catholic theo-logian N. P. Williams, Fellow and Chaplain of Exeter (and, from 1927, Lady Margaret Professor of Divinity and Canon of Christ Church). Fisher later recalled this man who was intellectually, theologically, and tempera-mentally so different from himself: Williams "was a very great scholar." But he was also "a very shy, frightened man who crept about the College, and when you talked to him he kept his eyes almost shut. He had a queer way of speaking as though he was saying prunes and prisms all the time."[18] Theologically, Fisher was more drawn to the evangelicals, although he did not share their enthusiasm for emotional conversion experiences. As a bud-ding ecumenist, he was attracted to the efforts of those men—especially John R. Mott (1865–1955) and Joseph Oldham (1874–1969)—who were working to draw the world's churches closer together in faith and mission.[19]

By the time Fisher left Oxford in the summer of 1911, he had ob-served the full range of church parties within Anglicanism. In church-manship, he was then what he would be for the rest of his ecclesiastical days: a centrist, leaning slightly toward the Low Church Protestant wing, but—both by deep-seated personal inclination and on principle—averse to party affiliation. A prayer-book Anglican, he respected the best features of both the Protestant and the Catholic emphases within the church, but he disliked the problems that extremists on either wing could cause by their exclusivist notions that they had special keys to the truth. His own judgment was that the evangelicals and the Anglo-Catholics represented positions that were not contradictory but complementary—"provided that," in his words, "the holders of these views never allow themselves to become militant or political. That destroys everything."[20]

Marlborough College (1911–1914)

Upon graduating, Geoffrey Fisher turned down offers from two colleges to begin his professional career in the University of Oxford. He knew that this sort of life was not the right one for him. He did not care to spend his time, as he put it, "correcting somebody else's answers"; and he did not

18. Quoted in ibid., 13.

19. Ibid., 14.

20. Ibid., 14; Purcell, *Fisher of Lambeth*, 67 (quotation); De-la-Noy, *Michael Ramsey,* 52.

want to pursue a subject—academic theology—that would mean having "to go on asking questions to which there was no answer."[21] And so he accepted an offer from Frank Fletcher, the head of Marlborough College, to return to the school as a member of its teaching staff. Fletcher had been a significant influence on Geoffrey when he was a student there. A first-rate instructor, Fletcher encouraged his students to learn to think for themselves.[22]

Fisher spent three happy years at his alma mater, proving to be a successful teacher, an effective disciplinarian, and an eager participant in all aspects of school life. He had no thought of leaving or of doing anything else, no burning ambition to rise higher. But then something happened that, mutatis mutandis, would happen again thirty years later: William Temple's old job became available and Geoffrey Fisher emerged as a leading candidate to fill it. In 1914 the post was the headmastership of Repton, a top-tier British public school located in Derbyshire, in central England. Founded as a charity school in 1557, by the middle of the nineteenth century it had become, in the words of one educational historian, "a fee-paying school catering to the needs of a burgeoning, *arriviste* middle class."[23]

William Temple had accepted a call to be rector of St. James's, Piccadilly, a prominent parish in London. When consulted by Geoffrey Fisher, both he and Frank Fletcher—now headmaster of Charterhouse—advised him to proceed with an application for the vacancy at Repton. In fact, both men had already discussed Fisher's potential as a headmaster and were keen on his appointment. After a fairly relaxed session with the school's governors, Fisher was offered the post. He accepted, and remained at the school for the next 18 years. Having been ordained deacon in 1912 and presbyter in 1913 after a short period of study (one term in the long vacation of 1911) at Wells Theological College, he was able to serve Repton as a priest-headmaster, a dual capacity that he believed essential to his ability to superintend all aspects of the school's life.[24]

21. Quoted in Carpenter, *Archbishop Fisher*, 15.

22. *DNB 1971–1980*, s.v. "Fisher, Geoffrey Francis, Baron Fisher of Lambeth."

23. Gronn, "An Experiment in Political Education," 2.

24. Carpenter, *Archbishop Fisher*, 16–17, 26; Purcell, *Fisher of Lambeth*, 49; Iremonger, *William Temple, Archbishop of Canterbury*, 154.

Repton (1914–1932)

Only two months after his appointment as headmaster in June 1914, Geoffrey Fisher had to confront problems caused by the outbreak of the First World War: a diminished teaching staff, incompetent replacements, and anxiety and restlessness among the boys. Sixty of the older students had already left to join the army, and six masters had also volunteered for war service.[25]

Fisher would have had enough to do merely finding his feet and taking on these special wartime challenges. But he also had to deal with the situation left behind by his predecessor, whose four years as headmaster were not an unalloyed success. William Temple had been a vital presence at Repton—religiously inspiring and intellectually stimulating—but he left the school with some serious deficiencies, particularly in the areas of organization and discipline. "I doubt if headmastering is really my line," he admitted to his brother.[26]

Relishing the mundane details of administrative tasks, Fisher plunged into the work of structural renovation. More so than most institutions, boarding schools live by their daily and weekly schedules. Like his predecessor, the new headmaster knew next to nothing about the natural sciences, but he recognized that science courses require not only reasonably up-to-date equipment but also sufficient time for laboratory experiments. Thus he made sure that the labs were properly outfitted, and from the ground up he constructed a new timetable, one that incorporated double periods for lab exercises. He also moved quickly, by expulsions and by the promulgation and enforcement of carefully spelled-out rules, to restore order among the boys.[27]

His own assured demeanor helped, for a headmaster could not be seen as wishy-washy. Just as Fisher made it clear to the boys who was on the right side in the world war ("[W]e are fighting for God's cause against the devil's"), so he had no difficulty making it clear who possessed sole authority to write and apply the rules.[28] In particular, during his first year, he moved ruthlessly to stamp out homosexual practices.[29] His actions, he

25. Palmer, *A Class of Their Own*, 157.

26. William Temple, letter to his brother, October 1910, quoted in Iremonger, *William Temple*, 128.

27. Palmer, *A Class of Their Own*, 163; Carpenter, *Archbishop Fisher*, 17–19; Purcell, *Fisher of Lambeth*, 54.

28. Carpenter, *Archbishop Fisher*, 18 (quotation), 19.

29. Palmer, *A Class of Their Own*, 158.

believed, quickly transformed the school: "Very soon," he said, "so far as one could tell, the thing was gone; and years afterwards, after I had left, a parent who was a boy under me said to someone else, and it reached me, that in his day while there was dirty talk still, nobody would have dreamt of going any further than that."[30]

The Roald Dahl Controversy

An Old Reptonian, Roald Dahl, the author of *Charlie and the Chocolate Factory*, caused a Fisher-related sensation when he claimed in his 1984 memoir, *Boy: Tales of Childhood*, that Geoffrey Fisher had been a sadistic flogger while headmaster of Repton. In *Boy* Dahl remembers that "[t]he Headmaster . . . struck me as being a rather shoddy bandy-legged little fellow with a big bald head and lots of energy but not much charm." Probably many of the boys would have offered a similar description, but then Dahl goes on to say that Fisher "used to deliver the most vicious beatings to the boys under his care."[31] Dahl provides an example of one of these terrible incidents. His best friend, Michael, told him about a merciless beating he was subjected to by Fisher, who paused every now and then to fill and light his pipe and "to lecture the kneeling boy about sin and wrongdoing."[32] After the flogging, the story goes, Fisher handed "the victim" a sponge, a basin, and a clean towel, and told him "to wash away the blood before pulling up his trousers."[33]

Dahl says that this brutal treatment caused him to "begin to have doubts about religion and even about God. If this person, I kept telling myself, was one of God's chosen salesmen on earth, then there must be something very wrong about the whole business." He could scarcely reconcile the Christian preacher of love with the ruthless headmaster: "I would sit in the dim light of the school chapel and listen to him preaching about the Lamb of God and about Mercy and Forgiveness . . . and my young mind would become totally confused," for he knew (or thought he knew) "that only the night before this preacher had shown neither Forgiveness nor Mercy in flogging some small boy who had broken the rules."[34]

Dahl's biographer, Jeremy Treglown, has pointed out, however, that the incident Dahl describes took place in May 1933, one year after Fisher

30. GF Papers, MS. 3467, fol. 37.
31. Dahl, *Boy: Tales of Childhood*, 130.
32. Ibid., 131.
33. Ibid., 132.
34. Ibid.

left Repton. The headmaster that administered this beating was John T. Christie, Fisher's successor. "If Dahl got his sadists mixed up," Treglown adds, "he also gives the impression that the beating was purely arbitrary. . . . In fact, the offender, who was almost eighteen and a house prefect, had been caught in bed with a younger boy."[35] Treglown notes that when Dahl's memoir came out, Archbishop Fisher was dead, but members of his family as well as many Old Reptonians were still alive, and they complained about the way in which Dahl had portrayed Fisher.[36]

Treglown acknowledges, however, that Dahl may have had a point regarding the customary harshness of Fisher's methods: "While some of [Dahl's] contemporaries remember Fisher as a great and good man," who was liked by all the boys, "others say that even by the standards of the day he was a severe head."[37] Treglown cites his interview with Stuart Hampshire, for example: "Fisher was very strict, Hampshire says, if not abnormally so, judged by the standards of the time. 'He was very unfeeling and illiberal,' and he certainly beat boys excessively—'by which I don't mean too often but too hard.'"[38] The next head, Christie, is remembered as having been much worse than Fisher. Following his move to Westminster in 1937, he became known, Treglown says, "for his learning, his piety, and his savagery."[39] Dahl's biographer also mentions that the boys, not the masters, administered most of the violence at Repton and at other public schools, and that as a student Roald Dahl himself could sometimes be sadistic and bullying.[40]

The Victor Gollancz Controversy

In the history of this period at Repton, Dahl's story of Fisher the brutal flogger has its counterpart in the story of Fisher the narrow-minded edu-

35. Treglown, *Roald Dahl,* 24–25.

36. In a book published in 1997, Palmer notes that "[t]he incorrect [i.e., Dahl's] version of the story had caused a minor sensation on its appearance ten years earlier [than the publication of Treglown's biography of Dahl]. Members of the Archbishop's family had been justifiably outraged at this slur on his memory, and they and a number of Old Reptonians complained to Dahl—who was, apparently, unrepentant." Palmer, *A Class of Their Own,* 165.

37. Treglown, *Roald Dahl,* 25.

38. Ibid., 25. Treglown is quoting from a telephone interview that he conducted with Sir Stuart Hampshire. See also Gollancz, *More for Timothy,* 148–49.

39. Treglown, *Roald Dahl,* 25.

40. Ibid., 26, 27. See Palmer, *A Class of Their Own,* 160–61, 163; and De-la-Noy, *Michael Ramsey,* 51.

cator. This account also involves someone who later became well known through book publishing: Victor Gollancz (1893–1967). Fisher's principal biographer refers to "the Gollancz-Somervell row" as a "remarkable" story.[41] Given its historical context, however, this little episode instead seems rather unremarkable, even drab and inconclusive.

The story begins with one of the problems mentioned at the outset of this section: the shortage of teachers owing to so many young men volunteering for the armed forces. In early 1916, needing to fill a vacancy in classics, Fisher turned to an employment agency for help and came up with Gollancz, a 22-year-old subaltern in the army who, because of poor eyesight, had been rejected for combat duty and assigned to Home Service with the Northumberland Fusiliers. Nine years older than Gollancz, David C. Somervell was the senior history master at Repton. Together they developed an idea for a new elective in the curriculum, a course that they believed would help students to understand the roots of the present conflict. With their headmaster's consent, they began in 1917 to teach a civics class—not a boring one on how the various units of government function but an exciting one that tackled contemporary political and social issues: imperialism, militarism, capitalism compared to socialism, and so on. This course was to be an early experiment in relevance.[42]

As a teacher, Gollancz was intellectually dazzling; Somervell was more reserved but also possessed of a remarkable mind. In some ways they made, in the words of a chronicler of their educational partnership, "a curious alliance: the young, vibrant and pulsating Gollancz; the measured, sober and circumspect Somervell. But the mercurial Gollancz and the rigorous Somervell were to prove a formidable combination."[43] Their civics class, launched in January 1917, grew increasingly popular with the students of the Upper Sixth Form. The following June, they published the first issue of a course-related newspaper, *A Public School Looks at the World*, which Fisher had also given his approval for. Although it ran for only five issues over nine months (until March 1918), this newspaper, which the students called the *Pubber*, proved to be more of a problem than the class.[44]

41. Carpenter, *Archbishop Fisher*, 20.

42. Gollancz and Somervell, *Political Education at a Public School*, chaps. 1–4; Gollancz, *More for Timothy*, 239–40; Edwards, *Victor Gollancz*, 95–109.

43. Gronn, "An Experiment," 6.

44. Edwards, *Victor Gollancz*, 112–15; Carpenter, *Archbishop Fisher*, 20–21; Purcell, *Fisher of Lambeth*, 55–56; Gronn, "An Experiment," 5–9; Gollancz, *More for Timothy*, 264–65.

Eventually outsiders caught wind of what was going on at Repton and asked pointed questions about the school's apparent pacifism. Not only senior masters at the school but also residents of Repton village began to voice their opposition to academic policies and practices that might undermine morale even as Reptonians were dying in the trenches. The headmaster received indications that the War Office was also concerned about what was happening at the school and indeed might decide to withdraw the government's recognition and funding of the Repton Officer Training Corps. Years after her husband's death, Lady Fisher recalled that if the War Office had terminated the school's OTC program, then "of course [this action] would have finished Repton because nobody would have sent a boy there in those days who couldn't get into an O.T.C."[45]

Perhaps worst of all from the point of view of a headmaster, Gollancz and his allies provoked not only dissent but also factional divisions and animosities within the school: master versus master, student versus student. In front of the boys, Gollancz, who in July 1916 had been warned by Fisher not to become too chummy with the lads, openly ridiculed and taunted faculty colleagues. Also, apparently with Gollancz's approval, one of his student protégés, an editor of the *Pubber*, had the paper sold at a radical bookseller's, Henderson & Sons, in Charing Cross Road, London, an establishment familiarly known as "the Bomb Shop." This incident exacerbated tensions by making the Repton situation more widely known outside the school. It probably increased the War Office's suspicions of Victor Gollancz's pacifist leanings. The last issue of the paper even listed Henderson's as a co-publisher. Finally, the headmaster, who had gone along with the experiments in liberal education and even praised these ventures at a number of points, decided that Gollancz had to go. Fisher could not risk further damage to his school's reputation, particularly during such a fraught period. Between the outbreak of war in 1914 and December 1917, the names of 247 Old Reptonians had been read out in chapel as among the fallen—roughly the equivalent of two-thirds of the total student body in any one year.[46]

Decades after they had squared off against one another, each of the principals in this conflict could speak well of the other man. Fisher called Gollancz brilliant and idealistic—though "not yet at all aware as to how

45. Letter from Lady Fisher to Gronn, October 27, 1983, in Gronn, "An Experiment," 17. See Palmer, *A Class of Their Own*, 177.

46. Edwards, *Victor Gollancz*, 121–22; Carpenter, *Archbishop Fisher*, 21–22; Gronn, "An Experiment," 13–18; Palmer, *A Class of Their Own*, 177; Gollancz, *More for Timothy*, chaps. 4–5.

to be a respectable idealist in such a community as a school."[47] And the publisher gratefully acknowledged that his old boss had given him an opportunity—to launch the civics class and the newspaper—that few other headmasters in that era would have provided.[48] In July 1940, James R. Darling, who had been a student editor of the *Pubber* and was now headmaster of Geelong Grammar School in Australia, told his brother-in-law, "It isn't easy running a school in war time. I have much more sympathy for Fisher than I ever had before and have meditated writing him an apology . . . for my failure to understand when I was at school."[49]

Accomplishments

Fisher's achievements during his years at Repton were many, but surely his most important accomplishment was his marriage in 1917 to Rosamond Chevallier Forman; together they would build a happy and close-knit family. Her father, the Reverend Arthur Francis Emilius Forman, had been a Repton housemaster until his premature death in 1905. Her grandfather was Steuart Adolphus Pears, who as headmaster of Repton between 1854 and 1874 did so much to transform it into one of Britain's leading public schools that he became known to history as the second founder.[50] Eventually Geoffrey and Rosamond Fisher had six sons, all born while the family was at Repton; each son went on to a career of noteworthy achievement. Rosamond enthusiastically entered into the life of the school and of the community. A gracious, devout, and attractive young woman, Rosamond was a prop and a mainstay to Geoffrey Fisher, and so she would remain wherever they went.[51]

Besides this achievement, Fisher successfully carried on the work of the school: restoring old buildings (most notably the medieval priory), hiring a superior faculty, doing some teaching and advising, and generally

47. GF Papers, MS. 3467, fol. 40. In the same statement, Fisher says of himself: "Gollancz was 24. I was 30. I was still, as a matter of fact, as flexible in outlook as Gollancz was . . . but rather more sober."

48. Gollancz, *More for Timothy*, 309.

49. J. R. Darling to R. LeFleming, July 17, 1940, quoted in Gronn, "An Experiment," 21. Revived after the war, the civics class was guided between 1920 and 1932 by a steadier hand: that of the Reverend Henry Balmforth, a High Church Anglican whose encouragement and influence proved important to a Repton student named Michael Ramsey, who succeeded his old headmaster in the Chair of St. Augustine of Canterbury. De-la-Noy, *Michael Ramsey*, 50.

50. See Thomas, *Repton, 1557–1957*, chap. 2.

51. Purcell, *Fisher of Lambeth*, 57–59.

in both academics and athletics helping Repton to thrive, which it did in the 1920s, prospering in the post-war boom that benefited other public schools as well.[52] Repton produced a commendable number of scholarship winners at Oxford and Cambridge. In 1921 the curriculum underwent a significant modification to allow more time for specialized study by boys of superior ability.[53] Throughout this period, Fisher proved his mettle as a headmaster: he "remained in the background," a biographer has written, "the efficient administrator waving his organizational wand to ensure the smooth functioning of the school."[54]

Fisher regularly spoke in chapel, preaching basic Christian doctrine and ethics to his young charges. His sermons were, if not brilliant like his predecessor's, at least meet for the occasion; they tended to stress aspects of practical morality for daily living, such as the Christian use of money.[55] In his talks with individual students, Fisher knew how to say the right word to buoy up the diffident or frightened boy. And, years after his service at Repton was over, he made a comment which revealed that he also understood how to talk with the brighter and more-confident lads: "They were a joy because they were so easy to talk to if you were prepared to discuss anything with them without . . . embarrassment. . . . It meant argument, endless argument, and all the fun of the chase."[56]

Besides the ecclesiastic Arthur Michael Ramsey, the outstanding graduates of Repton during Fisher's headmastership included the writer Christopher Isherwood and the church historian Charles Smyth, among many others. Ramsey's biographer, Owen Chadwick, has written of his subject's admiration for Fisher as a teacher of classical languages: "Fisher had zest. He rushed them along. He did not delay boringly on points of scholarship. He bubbled along with enthusiasm and humour. He made the dead languages into living literature."[57] In his last school report on Michael Ramsey, the headmaster wrote perceptively of the future archbishop: "A boy with plenty of force of character who, in spite of certain uncouthnesses, has done good service on his own lines."[58] Charles Smyth recalled the influence that Fisher could have through his informal com-

52. Thomas, *Repton*, 109.

53. Ibid., 109–110.

54. Palmer, *A Class of Their Own*, 181.

55. Ibid., 167.

56. GF Papers, MS. 3467, fol. 55.

57. Chadwick, *Michael Ramsey*, 11.

58. Ibid., 15.

ments—remarks that helped to train up a boy in the Anglican way: "I constantly remember things that he said in casual conversation which cumulatively taught me to understand, as nothing else outside of parochial experience has done, the nature and ethos of the Church of England."[59]

Geoffrey Fisher was an effective head of school. Possessing the essential ability to balance the near and the distant, he could handle a welter of details in an efficient manner while holding in mind the larger strategic plan. When Fisher stepped down as headmaster of Repton, William Temple said of him: "His skill and efficiency was subordinated to clear educational principles and high idealism."[60] No doubt Fisher was aided by the fact that he did not have to revitalize a financially struggling institution or spend endless hours on fundraising. The school's reputation when he arrived was so strong that, after the war, he had little trouble attracting good students and first-rate instructors.[61] Clearly Repton thought well of him. After his eighteen years of service, he continued to influence the school first as a member of the board of governors and then as its chairman.[62]

59. Smyth, "G.F.F.: An Appreciation," in Thomas, *Repton,* 114.

60. Quoted in Thomas, *Repton,* 112.

61. Charles Smyth has noted that a headmaster's choice of faculty members is crucial to the success of a school: "Part of the explanation of the Archbishop's success as a headmaster, and of the fact that these were vintage years in the history of Repton, is the self-evident truth that he possessed this flair [for choosing masters] in an exceptional degree. The scholarship lists . . . reflect the wisdom of his [choices]." Smyth, "G.F.F.: An Appreciation," in Thomas, *Repton,* 113.

62. Thomas, *Repton,* 104.

2

Chester and London: 1932–1945

Bishop of Chester (1932–1939)

B Y 1932 Geoffrey Fisher had been at Repton for eighteen years, and, with his characteristically good sense of timing, he knew he was ready for a change. He felt that parochial ministry—preferably, a rural bene-fice—would provide the best occupation for his personality and strengths. But those who were familiar with his work at Repton, particularly with his outstanding administrative skills, believed that he was well suited to be a bishop.

William Temple, who had become archbishop of York in 1929, con-sidered the diocese of Chester (more or less equivalent to the county of Cheshire) to be the right one—both in churchmanship and in its varied town-and-country ministry—to engage the talents and interests of his successor at Repton. Therefore he urged Fisher upon Cosmo Gordon Lang, the archbishop of Canterbury. Lang wrote to the premier, Ramsey MacDonald, providing the names of the men he thought best qualified for the Chester bishopric. The archbishop of Canterbury had two names bracketed in the first spot on his list: Fisher's and that of Nugent Hicks, the bishop of Gibraltar (responsible for Anglican churches in Southern Europe). In due course the prime minister selected Fisher for the post (Hicks would shortly be appointed bishop of Lincoln), and in early May he notified Fisher that he intended to submit his name to the Crown to succeed Luke Paget. The King approved Fisher's appointment, and on May 14 it was made public.[1]

Frank Fletcher, Fisher's old boss at Marlborough College and now headmaster of Charterhouse, wrote to him to say that he thought that this "promotion" was the right move: it would "involve *harder* work, something

---

1. Carpenter, *Archbishop Fisher*, 29–30; Palmer, *A Class of Their Own*, 182.

that would really extend" his former protégé.[2] On September 21, 1932, at York Minster, Geoffrey Fisher was consecrated bishop of Chester.

Notice that when he became a bishop, Geoffrey Fisher had never been a parish priest. Moreover, as headmaster of Repton, he largely confined his activities to the work of the school and therefore did not attract much attention outside it. His appointment to the bishopric of Chester came as a surprise to many. He was going into a diocese that was unfamiliar to him and where he was unknown by the people. It comprised 300 priests, some of whom resented their new bishop for his lack of parochial experience. But Fisher's administrative work as a schoolmaster served him in good stead. He always felt that the tasks of a headmaster and those of a diocesan bishop were similar.[3]

His greatly admired predecessor had not been a notably effective administrator, and so Fisher set out to put diocesan organization and finances to rights. He enjoyed excellent relations with the cathedral dean (Frank Selwyn Macaulay Bennett, who had done so much to make the cathedral an active, welcoming center of religious life[4]), with the archdeacons of Chester and Macclesfield, and with the rural deans, who were the vital links between the parish clergy in the various localities and the diocese.

Fisher's good humor and his intelligent commitment to duty carried him far. Early in his episcopate, in the autumn of 1933, he lent his support to an evangelistic crusade sponsored by the Industrial Christian Fellowship Mission, preaching in the evenings in the slums of Birkenhead. To increase the financial support of inadequately funded congregations and their clergy, he labored to establish the Bishop's Appeal Fund. In a debate in the Church Assembly, he successfully argued on behalf of the maintenance of a diocesan institution threatened with closure: the Church Training College in Chester, which also served the dioceses of Manchester, Liverpool, and Blackburn. And he warmly embraced his official visitations: at confirmations and institutions he spent time with the people, talking easily with all sorts and conditions of men, women, and children.

In a short while, both the clergy and the laypeople grew to like their friendly and capable, if occasionally rather authoritarian, bishop, and this response was reciprocated by Geoffrey and Rosamond Fisher. Indeed, the latter became diocesan president of the Mothers' Union (and later

2. Quoted in Carpenter, *Archbishop Fisher*, 30.
3. Purcell, *Fisher of Lambeth*, 65–66.
4. See Lloyd, *The Church of England, 1900–1965*, 392–99, 401–2.

its central president), and she used her own car to visit parishes all over Cheshire.[5]

Fisher's work in Chester and his characteristic manner of carrying it out revealed another essential component of his leadership besides intelligence and industry. Someone who knew him well, Ian H. White-Thomson, a former dean of Canterbury who also served as Fisher's chaplain at Lambeth, stresses his sheer resilience. As bishop of Chester, Fisher seemed incapable of ever letting intractable problems or fractious individuals get him down. "Among his chief qualities were his sense of humour, his imperturbability, his resilience, and his astonishing physical stamina. Short and sturdy in build, he seemed to exude energy and strength."[6]

Betokening a balanced blend of humility and self-confidence, this ability to bounce back and persevere no matter what suggests both a healthy ego and a bulldog determination that any would-be antagonists would have to take into account. In the event, his opponents in the Chester diocese were few. The parish clergy, including those who had questioned the fitness of a man who had never been an incumbent, were grateful not only for Fisher's mastery of episcopal administration but also for the warm personal concern he consistently displayed on their behalf.

Bishop of London (1939–1945)

The Call to London

His outstanding performance as bishop of Chester made Geoffrey Fisher someone to be thought of as soon as one of the most senior ecclesiastical posts became available. In the Church of England, the sees of Durham, London, and Winchester enjoyed a special prominence. They ranked higher than all others except for the two archiepiscopal sees, Canterbury in the southern province and York in the northern. Regardless of his seniority of consecration, a bishop of one of these three dioceses was entitled to sit in the House of Lords as soon as he took possession of his see. Among these three dioceses, London ranked first (followed by Durham). The two archbishops in England and the bishop of London always became members of the Privy Council. Moreover, this ancient see city was the capital of the British Empire, the center of finance and culture, and the hub of the

5. Carpenter, *Archbishop Fisher*, 32–52; Purcell, *Fisher of Lambeth*, 69–78; *DNB 1971–1980*, s.v. "Fisher, Geoffrey Francis, Baron Fisher of Lambeth."

6. *DNB 1971–1980*, s.v. "Fisher, Geoffrey Francis, Baron Fisher of Lambeth."

Anglican Communion: Lambeth Palace, Church House, various church party and voluntary society headquarters, the major church publishing houses, the most famous churches—all were in London.

When Arthur Foley Winnington-Ingram, who had been bishop of London since 1901, finally stepped down in 1939, he left behind an important but also troubled diocese, one that for many years had been allowed to run a bit wild. Indeed, the diocese was in just the sort of neglected state that Geoffrey Fisher was known among church leaders to be capable of putting right. Once again a jurisdiction cried out for someone who would bring order, and who better than this longtime headmaster and adroit diocesan to exercise the necessary discipline?

Fisher and Bishop Cyril Garbett of Winchester—who, at sixty-three, was twelve years Fisher's senior—quickly became the leading candidates for the London bishopric, although two other bishops—Kirk of Oxford and Rawlinson of Derby—were also under consideration. Winnington-Ingram thought that Fisher was the best man to succeed him—an opinion undoubtedly influenced by the fact that both men were Old Marlburians.[7] The story of how the bishop of Chester eventually received this appointment has two interesting features: the initial hesitancy of the prime minister in backing Fisher, and the hesitancy of the candidate in accepting the offer when it did come.

Archbishop Lang was in favor of Fisher, but the prime minister, Neville Chamberlain, had no decided preference. His concerns centered not on the quality of Fisher's intellect or administrative ability but on his spiritual character. Lang took up this matter with a friend, a canon missioner in the diocese of Chester, who offered reassuring testimony on behalf of his bishop. With this information in hand, Lang told the premier that he need not have any worries about Fisher's spiritual depth: "The Bishop is undoubtedly a man of genuine deep personal religion. His piety is that of the best type of English layman . . . rather than that of 'religious.'" Fisher's spirituality, the archbishop pointed out, is not readily apparent for two reasons: "he is very shy and humble about it (very English)," and "his other gifts of intellect and administration are vastly more obvious to the world."[8] Satisfied with this appraisal, Chamberlain moved forward with Fisher's nomination.[9]

7. Smyth, *Cyril Forster Garbett*, 237.
8. CGL Papers 169, fols. 241–42.
9. Palmer, *High and Mitred*, 210–11.

Upon receiving the prime minister's letter offering the bishopric and Lang's letter urging him to take it, Fisher was overcome by an uncustomary spell of doubt and indecision. "I knelt down and wept like a child," he wrote in his diary.[10] It was not that the offer had come as any kind of surprise. Rather, he was not certain in his own mind and heart that he could fulfill the requirements of this position. Various churchmen, including the dean of St. Paul's, assured him that he could. After much prayer during Good Friday and Holy Saturday of 1939, Fisher, too, was sufficiently convinced.[11]

It is not hard to see why he hesitated before the jump. To him London was unfamiliar territory, and what he knew of the ecclesiastical situation there was more than enough to give him pause. Comprising 600 parishes, the London diocese seemed unwieldy in size and unrestrained in its diversity. For the contentious extremism of its church parties, this diocese was notorious. A Fisher biographer has written that many clergy and laypeople in London "complained that there was a lack of order and general discipline in the parishes; . . . the Prayer Book was being ignored and . . . many a church was becoming an 'island refuge' for a bewildering variety of liturgical exiles."[12] Among the church societies that had their headquarters in the capital, one stood out as the most problematic: the Church Union, formed in 1934 by the amalgamation of the English Church Union and the Anglo-Catholic Congress. The Protestant wing of the Established Church also had its extremist section.[13]

Writing to Archbishop Temple while still trying to make up his mind, Fisher acknowledged his fears: yes, he had powers sufficient to the demands of a friendly diocese such as Chester was, but London was a mare's-nest. When called to speak on religious subjects, he could do well, but he was an amateur in spirituality and his resources in that line were quickly depleted. He was no intellectual and no statesman: he was uncomfortable with abstractions, and he disliked making the kinds of public pronouncements that people expected to hear from a bishop of London. In reply, Temple did not challenge this self-assessment, but he made clear his conviction that Fisher was the right man for London—he had the skills that were wanted—and that he had to accept this offer. By Easter Sunday Fisher was largely of the same mind. God, he considered, had been good to him.

---

10. Quoted in Palmer, *High and Mitred*, 211; Carpenter, *Archbishop Fisher*, 55–58.

11. Carpenter, *Archbishop Fisher*, 57–58; Matthews, *Memories and Meanings*, 217.

12. Carpenter, *Archbishop Fisher*, 60.

13. Purcell, *Fisher of Lambeth*, 79–81.

"Lovest thou me?" he remembered the Risen Lord saying to Simon Peter (John 21). If Geoffrey Fisher was truly grateful for what God had done in his life and if he trusted in God's mercy, then, he asked himself, how could he now turn aside from a clear call to feed God's sheep?[14]

Wartime

Fisher took up his new post on September 1, 1939. Two days later, Britain was at war with Germany. The long, quiet period known as the "phoney war" ended in mid-August 1940, when the German air attacks on London and other British cities began. The Blitz—a British colloquialism derived from *Blitzkrieg*, the German word for lightning war—fell on London every night but one between mid-September and mid-November. Other cities involved in war production—including Manchester, Sheffield, Coventry, Belfast, and Glasgow—also suffered. During 1940–1941, this aerial bombardment killed 42,000 men, women, and children in the United Kingdom. Over 139,000 were injured and approximately 1,000,000 houses destroyed. The effects of the Blitz took their toll on morale, but for many Londoners the attacks steeled their resolve and strengthened their sense of solidarity.

For the Fishers, life in Fulham Palace, the home of the bishops of London (until 1973), brought its own stresses. Even before it was bombed, the palace was in a shabby state, forcing its occupants to confine themselves to one wing. After the Blitz began, Rosamond Fisher felt compelled to abandon the episcopal residence, removing herself and her youngest boys to Minehead, in Somerset, where her mother lived.[15]

At the palace, the bishop of London experienced the air raids like everyone else in the capital. All were vulnerable. Fisher had a certain toughness of spirit that enabled him to soldier on, consistently, no matter what the circumstances. Residents of the palace slept in the house in improvised shelters, made as secure as possible by the placement of large beams and sandbags. In early September they could see the glow in the sky from the fires caused by incendiary bombs dropped on the London docks and on neighborhoods in east London along the bank. During the day Fisher worked according to an ad hoc schedule, trying to meet demands as they arose. He visited the East End, saw the demolished houses, and tried to bolster the confidence of the people and their clergy. Sometimes, following

14. Carpenter, *Archbishop Fisher*, 56–58.
15. Ibid., 63.

a bomb hit, he would help with the rescue work.[16] He told his wife how impressed he was by the "quiet heroism" and the "persistent humour" of ordinary Londoners.[17]

On one night during the Blitz—September 11—the bishop's residence accommodated 200 evacuees, babies to pensioners, bombed out of their houses in surrounding neighborhoods; the next night they were moved to a nearby school.[18] During the nights of September 25 and 26, Fulham Palace, which occupied a vulnerable spot along the River Thames (just west and north of Putney Bridge), was damaged by Luftwaffe raids, which had expanded beyond the East End to include other parts of London. Rosamond Fisher badly wanted to return home to London, but her husband, realizing the risk involved if both parents and their youngest children should be together in one place, would not let her leave her country retreat. Finally, at the end of September, her youngest boys having returned to school, Mrs. Fisher rejoined her husband. The couple's anxiety continued, however, as four of their sons were to serve in the army during the war, and one of them would be a POW in Italy for 18 months before escaping.[19]

Life at Fulham Palace would continue to be extraordinarily trying. Whenever part of the residence was seriously damaged by bomb blast, the area had to be closed off. If living quarters were damaged, then the occupants had to move to a portion of the house that had so far been spared. The bishop's secretary during this period later recalled that her boss "slept in an underground shelter beneath the Porteous Library, while Mrs. Fisher was in another part of the Palace. That was planned so that, if a direct hit were received, the risk of both parents being killed was at least halved."[20] The one exception to the palace sleeping arrangement was the customary practice of F. C. Synge, the bishop's chaplain, who slept on the lawn. Better to chance being hit by flying shrapnel, he mused (while lying outside on his camp bed?), than to risk being buried alive under a pile of palace rubble.[21]

It was Synge—who not only survived the war but also went on to become principal of Christchurch College, New Zealand—who insightfully

16. Ibid., 64; Purcell, *Fisher of Lambeth*, 85–86, 90.

17. Quoted in Carpenter, *Archbishop Fisher*, 65.

18. Ibid., 65–66; Purcell, *Fisher of Lambeth*, 84.

19. Carpenter, *Archbishop Fisher*, 66–68.

20. Marjorie Harry Salmon, quoted in Purcell, *Fisher of Lambeth*, 85.

21. Ibid., 82.

explained the source of the deep satisfaction that Fisher derived from completing each day, after lunch, *The Times* crossword puzzle. Through this activity, which was his "supreme recreation," Fisher for the moment could be both blissfully focused on a challenge and unusually carefree—because, unlike what awaited him, the daily puzzle was "an artificial problem." Exercising his faculties was "his delight and his calling"; being able to do so "without responsibility" was a peculiar joy. And indulging his penchant for the crossword prepared the bishop for what lay ahead: "throwing light upon dark confusion, organising, rearranging, making machinery work smoothly, solving problems of manpower or finances." These tasks he could apply himself to, "confident that (like the crossword puzzle) the solution was there to be found."[22]

One of the most important of these tasks concerned national reconstruction: not only the rebuilding but also the reorganization of church life in the many areas severely damaged by war. To this crucial matter the Church Assembly turned its attention. Officially called the National Assembly of the Church of England, the Church Assembly was—until its replacement by the General Synod in 1970—the chief deliberative and legislative body of the Church of England. It consisted of the House of Bishops and the House of Clergy, who were the members respectively of the two Upper and the two Lower Houses of Convocation of the Provinces of Canterbury and York, and of the House of Laity, who were laymen elected by the diocesan laity. Under the Enabling Act of 1919, the Legislative Committee of the Church Assembly had the authority to submit church-related measures to the Ecclesiastical Committee of Parliament. This committee comprised 15 members of the House of Lords nominated by the Lord Chancellor and 15 members of the House of Commons nominated by the Speaker of the House of Commons. If the Ecclesiastical Committee cleared the proposed legislation, then it went to Parliament, which could either accept or reject—but not amend—the proposal. If accepted, then the measure received the Royal Assent and became law.[23]

Which is what happened to both the Diocesan Reorganisation Committee Measure 1941 and the Reorganisation Areas Measure 1943, although the route leading to their final approval was long and full of challenges. Having been appointed by the Church Assembly to chair the

22. Synge, quoted in ibid., 87.

23. The Enabling Act is officially known as the Church of England Assembly (Powers) Act 1919. "The Enabling Act, 1919," in Flindall, *The Church of England, 1815–1948*, 342–43; *ODCC*, 3rd ed., s.v. "Church Assembly"; Garbett, *Church and State in England*, 115; idem, *The Claims of the Church of England*, 193.

Archbishops' War Damage Committee, which initiated this legislation, Geoffrey Fisher played the leading role throughout this process. Set up in late 1940, this committee comprised, in addition to its chairman, eight clergy and four laymen. It was, in particular, an ecclesiastical response to the War Damage Act of 1940, which recognized that the Nazis' serial bombing of British cities had caused such extensive devastation that local authorities and private institutions alone could not be expected to take on the massive work of reconstruction. This situation called for a much wider view and for a truly comprehensive effort of planning and rebuilding.[24]

The War Damage Act spurred the various church bodies—the Roman Catholics, the Anglicans, and the Free Churches—to plan in a correspondingly thoughtful and all-encompassing fashion. They needed to take into account the fact that not everything that had been lost could—or should—be replaced. It might make little sense, for example, to rebuild a huge edifice in a neighborhood that already had more churches than it could support. Thus the disaster of war presented a horrendous problem but also an opportunity for the restructuring of ministry. In the House of Lords, Geoffrey Fisher made exactly this point in 1940: "In London and other great cities there are whole districts in which hardly a church remains untouched. It is neither possible nor desirable that a very large destroyed church should be rebuilt as it was and where it was." The reason was that "[c]onditions have changed, old needs have disappeared, new needs have been created and in many parts of our great cities there were before the war too many separate parishes and too many churches."[25]

The reorganization measures for which Fisher and his committee eventually won approval helped the dioceses of the church to negotiate claims for compensation, to strategize with greater freedom, to deploy resources appropriately, and, if necessary, to reconfigure the shape of ministry in damaged areas, even if that meant adjusting parish boundaries, reallocating endowments, or holding benefices in plurality.[26] Fisher's committee carved out a path for the future: showing how parishes could be yoked together, ministries teamed, and incomes redirected, with monies channeled by the Church Commissioners through diocesan funds to parishes as needed.[27]

24. Carpenter, *Archbishop Fisher*, 69.

25. Quoted in ibid., 69.

26. Ibid., 70–77.

27. Purcell, *Fisher of Lambeth*, 101–2; see Garbett, *Church and State in England*, 283–88. The Church Commissioners were formed in 1948 by an amalgamation of the Ecclesiastical Commissioners and Queen Anne's Bounty.

At the end of the one and one-quarter hours that it took Fisher to unfold the Reorganisation Areas Measure before the Church Assembly, William Temple, who presided over this meeting, told him how well he had succeeded not only in clearly presenting the complex material but also in holding everyone's attention throughout his lengthy explanation.[28] The work of the Archbishops' War Damage Committee—difficult and painstaking, but successfully completed—brought the bishop of London with his top-flight administrative skills and fair and equable manner increased recognition in the Church of England. It was really his first turn in the spotlight of the national church, although he was still not widely known when he became archbishop of Canterbury in 1945. His committee service was arduous, then, but useful. From this complex work he learned a great deal about the customs—not only the procedures but also the folkways—of the Church Assembly. As Edward Carpenter has written, chairing this important committee was undoubtedly a constructive learning experience for someone who was soon to preside at the sessions of the Church Assembly—"a role which, though it irritated Cosmo Lang and bored William Temple, delighted Geoffrey Fisher."[29] This legislative achievement was also beneficial to the Church of England and to the bishop of London as a harbinger of things to come, for Fisher was to be an active leader of the postwar effort to modernize the Church of England.[30]

Fisher chaired other important, war-related committees as well. In December 1940 he established his own committee to look out for the architectural treasures of the City of London. This committee established procedures for churches to follow if they were damaged by bomb attacks, it instituted measures to salvage valuable artifacts, and it made decisions regarding plans for individual churches that had been bombed.[31] He also chaired the Churches' Main War Damage Committee, which reached across ecclesiastical boundaries to include representatives of other church bodies—from Roman Catholics on the right wing of the liturgical spectrum to Baptists on the left. By coordinating and presenting churches' claims for compensation under the War Damage Act, this committee provided assistance to the War Damage Commission.[32]

28. Purcell, *Fisher of Lambeth*, 101–2.

29. Carpenter, *Archbishop Fisher*, 77.

30. Purcell, *Fisher of Lambeth*, 104.

31. Carpenter, *Archbishop Fisher*, 78–83.

32. Purcell, *Fisher of Lambeth*, 102–4.

In the autumn of 1939, upon becoming bishop of London, Geoffrey Fisher was asked by Archbishop Cosmo Lang to chair the Archbishops' War Committee. This committee had a rather vague but nonetheless important charge. Modern war generated its own peculiar questions and problems; the committee was to consider those matters that directly affected the church. Its members included the bishops with sees in or near London. One regular topic involved the Home Guard. Their commanding officers tended to schedule their training on Sunday mornings, making it impossible for those who wanted to attend divine worship to do so. Might not the 11 a.m. training be rescheduled, if at all possible? The director-general of the Home Guard issued instructions along the lines proposed by Bishop Fisher.[33]

Another example of the sort of question that came up: May the military use church towers as lookout posts or even as places to mount anti-aircraft guns? Yes to the former, replied Anthony Eden, the secretary of war: With invasion by the Nazis a real threat, church towers might be especially useful in this period (the summer of 1940) for spotting enemy parachutists or troop-carrying aircraft. But no to the latter: the church officials need not worry about the towers being used for machine guns or other weapons. Not all questions were decisively answered: What if the observer carried a rifle into the tower?[34]

Complicated issues arose which were often hard to resolve: troubling matters, for example, having to do with the occupation of consecrated ground by local units of the Home Guard. Because these units' actions were not always in strict compliance with the regulations issued by the Home Office, the same sorts of problems tended to recur. Parish priests were naturally distressed to find military forces using churchyards for gun emplacements and digging up hallowed ground for defense works. Fisher strongly protested against the use of holy ground for profane purposes, sent Eden a set of safeguards designed to prevent future problems, and received a reply that only partially met his demands: Eden could not order procedures to be followed (such as obtaining the prior consent of both the incumbent and the diocesan registrar) which might cause dangerous delays.[35]

Many other matters—from bishops' petrol rationing, to coupons required for vestments, to blackout regulations for early-morning Christmas

33. Carpenter, *Archbishop Fisher*, 85–86.

34. Ibid., 87–89.

35. Ibid., 89–90.

services—came before the Archbishops' War Committee. One particularly interesting question concerned the extent to which clergy might actively participate in war-related duties. Some Anglican clergy wanted to join the Home Guard. Fisher said that the Bench of Bishops did not wish to encourage clergy to do this but could not forbid them either, as long as they fulfilled their pastoral duties.[36]

Disorder in the Diocese

The Second World War presented uniquely exigent demands, but, year in and year out, being a father in God to his clergy was every bishop's chief pastoral concern. Before Fisher took over the diocese from his predecessor, Winnington-Ingram invited him to Fulham Palace and indicated that he would like to tell him everything he needed to know about his new post. It was a short lesson, Fisher later recalled: "We are just one gloriously happy family," the bishop of London assured him. "Of course you and I are both Marlburians, and we are used to meeting unusual situations. But that will be all right, my boy; just carry on and all will be well."[37]

The actual ecclesiastical situation was more complicated—and more worrisome—than Winnington-Ingram revealed to anyone, including himself. He "had retired in a rosy glow of sentiment," writes William Purcell. "But in terms of the true condition of his diocese, he had by then long parted company with reality."[38] Because of the concentration in London of the leadership of the more-extreme church parties, this bishopric, in the words of another observer, was "certainly no sinecure," even in peacetime.[39] Under Fisher's mild-mannered predecessor, discipline—normally imposed through episcopal oversight—had been weak for years, with clergy openly dissenting from the provisions of the prayer book. Upon Fisher's arrival, the diocese was divided, confused, and unhappy.[40]

The new bishop attempted to improve discipline by issuing a series of pronouncements on acceptable liturgical practice. The principal concerns centered on the extreme Anglo-Catholics' unauthorized departures from the prayer book, especially in relation to the service of Holy Communion,

36. Ibid., 92–93.

37. Quoted in Purcell, *Fisher of Lambeth*, 81.

38. Ibid., 81. Winnington-Ingram attempted to forbid benediction with a monstrance, but many Anglo-Catholic clergy simply refused to accept his regulations. See Yates, *Anglican Ritualism*, 350–51.

39. Staples, "Archbishop Geoffrey Francis Fisher: An Appraisal," 242.

40. Purcell, *Fisher of Lambeth*, 94.

which they customarily called the Mass. From the beginning of the twentieth century, controversy revolved around a particular Anglo-Catholic ritual known as Benediction. Following the practice of the ancient church, Anglicans have often (though not always) said that the consecrated bread and wine could be "reserved" for the communion of the sick and for similar weighty causes. Disputes arose over the appropriateness and therefore the permissibility of private devotions and public rituals centered on this consecrated bread and wine, which was typically held in a tabernacle on the altar or in an aumbry in the wall of the sanctuary.

A service of public devotion to the Reserved Sacrament, Benediction (or Adoration) was not provided for in the prayer book. Understood by those who practiced it as a ritual means of expressing their faith in and their devotion to the sacramental presence of Christ in the Mass, this service involved the veneration of the Host exposed outside the service of Holy Communion. The reserved Host was removed from the tabernacle or aumbry, placed in a monstrance (a frame or vessel of gold or silver with a round window for displaying the consecrated bread), and censed. The service included prayers and hymns stressing Christ's real presence in the eucharistic elements. The culmination of the service was the blessing of the people with the Host: the priest held the Host in the monstrance and made the sign of the cross over the people. He then returned the Host to the tabernacle.

Through his Bishops' Regulations, Fisher made it clear where the church's bishops authorized deviations from the 1662 Book of Common Prayer (for example: in the Communion service, allowing the exhortation to be omitted or permitting a gradual hymn to be sung between readings from the Bible) and where the bishops did not authorize deviations (such as Benediction). In addition, through careful appointments to vacant livings he hoped gradually to gain a greater degree of obedience and conformity in the diocese, especially in those parishes which were liturgically the farthest out of line. Change came slowly, but by the time his tenure of office ended in 1945, he had made a bit of headway. At least all the clergy in the diocese of London were aware of what the official standards were.[41]

Fisher was disappointed, however, that he had not been more successful in bringing about a fuller measure of discipline and respect for authority in the disordered diocese he had inherited. For the most part, the extreme Anglo-Catholic clergy continued to do as they liked, and securing agreement on proper liturgical boundaries was as elusive a goal as ever. For

41. Ibid., 95.

several reasons, however, this reality soon ceased to be quite as irksome as it had been. After the war, the liturgical movement brought about major changes in the worship lives of both Protestants and Roman Catholics, stimulating interest in the practices of the early church and making the decades-long battles between high and low Anglicans seem outdated. Many changes that now occurred were ones long advocated by Anglo-Catholic liturgical scholars. In addition, London churches increasingly drew on a self-selected clientele who were less likely to be confused or offended by what they found there. They attended a particular church not because it was their local parish church but because they liked its clergy and its distinctive style of worship. And the church as a whole largely moved on to fresh concerns—in theology, in social ethics, and in ecumenical relations with other church bodies.[42]

Ecumenism in Wartime

In the decades before the Second Vatican Council (1962–65), relations between the Roman Catholic Church and other ecclesial communities were typically difficult and often strained. Pope Leo XIII's bull *Apostolicae Curae* (1896) had declared Anglican orders invalid. Rome did not believe that the Anglican church was in the true apostolic succession; and of course Anglicans rejected key doctrines of the Roman Catholic Church, such as papal infallibility. As one church historian has written, "For Rome, the *Via Media Anglicana* was the worst of abominations. Not only had schismatics and heretics broken away with impunity—indeed, with triumphant success: here was also an uncomfortable rival, affirming itself to be both Catholic and Reformed."[43]

This estrangement between the Church of Rome and the Church of England was one reason why Archbishop Geoffrey Fisher's visit to Pope

42. Carpenter, *Archbishop Fisher*, 116–25. "The liturgical changes of the 1960s and 1970s resulted in an overall leveling-up of Anglican worship in general, though a leveling-down in those Anglo-Catholic churches that felt they ought to be more in line with mainstream developments, not just in their own church but in Western Christendom as a whole." Wearing eucharistic vestments and reserving the Blessed Sacrament no longer distinguished Anglo-Catholic parishes. See Yates, *Anglican Ritualism*, 368–71, 383 (quotation, 370–71).

Unauthorized departures from the Book of Common Prayer, particularly in Anglo-Catholic parishes in London, continued to be a concern for GF in the 1950s. Officially prohibited, Benediction was nonetheless still practiced. Fisher hoped that new canons and ecclesiastical courts would help remedy the problem. See GF Papers 73, fol. 387; 79, fols. 259–64; 93, fols. 308–14; 113, fols. 77–79.

43. Nichols, *The Politics of the Vatican*, 314.

John XXIII in 1960 was both a decidedly low-keyed affair and a momentous event: a quiet meeting remarkable for having occurred at all. It is also why the ecumenical engagement with the Sword of the Spirit was significant: at least as noteworthy for what it attempted as for what it accomplished.

Launched by the cardinal archbishop of Westminster, Arthur Hinsley (1865–1943), on August 1, 1940, the Sword of the Spirit was a large-scale campaign of the Church of Rome, although in its first year it also encouraged non-Roman Catholics to participate. It grew out of the recognition that the problems of society and of international relations were spiritual problems that the church must confront.[44] Through study, prayer, and action, this movement sought to promote international efforts on behalf of justice and concord among nations and peoples, thereby establishing the conditions for a lasting peace. The Sword of the Spirit derived its ethical marching orders both from traditional natural-law principles and from the five peace points of Pope Pius XII. Laid down in his Christmas Allocution of 1939, the pope's conditions for a just peace were founded on the right of every nation, no matter how small or weak, to life and independence, and on the right of every minority population within a nation to exist, with their basic freedoms intact. To advance these ends, Pius XII called for progressive disarmament—a disarming of the bellicose spirit as well as of war materiel—and the establishment of an international court.

As conceived by Cardinal Hinsley, the Sword of the Spirit was a weapon to be used to fight for justice both in the present conflict and in the peace that followed. The Sword's program declared a simple and stark contrast between the principles of Christianity and the values of all forms of totalitarianism, including Nazism. In the face of this totalitarian threat, the Sword sought to make clear what was at stake in the war. Totalitarian regimes struggle to impose an alternative way of life, one that opposes, as the Sword's executive committee put it, "all the natural rights that Christianity upholds—the rights of God, of man, of the family, of minorities, of dependent peoples." Therefore Christians must fight both for victory against this oppressor and for a "reconstruction of Europe . . . based upon these same natural and Christian principles."[45]

Proponents of the Sword understood the Second World War to be not merely a battle between competing national interests but also—in the words of Cardinal Hinsley's biographer, writing during the Second World

---

44. Hastings, *A History of English Christianity, 1920–2000*, 393–94.

45. Quoted in Heenan, *Cardinal Hinsley*, 183.

War—"a battle for the possession of the human soul."[46] For this reason, they said, the armaments of war must include what the New Testament refers to as "the sword which the Spirit gives you, the word of God," for the enemies are "cosmic powers . . . the authorities and potentates of this dark age." These words are from the sixth chapter of Ephesians, the key text for Cardinal Hinsley's interpretation of the underlying nature of this fight.[47] "We can never compromise," he said, "with any form of idolatrous absolutism, whatever be its name, communism, nazism or fascism."[48]

Leading British ecumenists such as Bishop George Bell of Chichester found this new cause thoroughly appealing. They recognized its potential for good and relished the ecumenical scope and possibilities of such a venture. The horrors of war and the hopes of such churchmen as Archbishop William Temple had brought Christians closer together, at least in spirit. Perhaps now was the time, for the sake of the future, to cooperate in a shared program for international peace and justice.[49]

The basic principles of the Sword of the Spirit were affirmed in a letter published in *The Times* on December 21, 1940—a letter signed not only by Cardinal Hinsley but also by the Moderator of the Free Church Federal Council (Walter H. Armstrong) and by the archbishops of Canterbury (Lang) and York (Temple). As guiding principles for national life and international relations, this statement cited and supported both the pope's peace points and the five standards of the Oxford Conference, an ecumenical meeting held in 1937 which had addressed social and political problems.[50] The specific content of this published letter mattered less than the fact of its production: "Such a letter was . . . wholly unprecedented," one church historian has noted. It was tangible evidence that "in face of the national emergency the ecumenical fraternity had widened . . . to include the cardinal archbishop of Westminster."[51]

These principles also received attention on May 10 and 11, 1941, when two well-attended public meetings were held: the first, on "A

46. Ibid., 184.

47. See the long quotation from Hinsley in Heenan, *Cardinal Hinsley*, 187. Hinsley called Eph 6:10–20 "the charter of the Movement"; quoted in Heenan, *Cardinal Hinsley*, 194.

48. Quoted in ibid., 195.

49. Jasper, *George Bell*, 250; Heenan, *Cardinal Hinsley*, 189.

50. The five standards were (1) the abolition of extreme inequality, (2) the right of every child to an education, (3) the defense of the family, (4) the restoration of a sense of divine vocation in each person's daily work, and (5) the careful use of the earth's resources as God's gifts to all human beings. Heenan, *Cardinal Hinsley*, 181.

51. Hastings, *History of English Christianity, 1920–2000*, 393–94.

Christian International Order," chaired by Cardinal Hinsley, and the second, on "A Christian Order in Britain," chaired by Archbishop Lang. The speakers—from the Church of England, the Roman Catholic Church, and the Free Churches—composed a strong bench. In addition to George Bell, they included such well-known names as Dorothy L. Sayers and Father Martin d'Arcy, S.J. Cardinal Hinsley was the major force behind this unusual inclusiveness. At the end of the first meeting, the cardinal archbishop, at Bell's suggestion, led the assembly in saying together the Lord's Prayer. But after this meeting he was taken to task by his fellow bishops for praying with non-Roman Catholics, who, when the organization's new constitution was adopted three months later, were excluded from full membership in the Sword of the Spirit.[52]

The Roman Catholic position was that a total merging of efforts with non-Roman Catholics would be dangerous and misleading. Many Roman Catholic bishops had been worried about the Sword from its inception. To them the character of its make-up was, Hastings writes, suspiciously "lay, ecumenical, intellectually progressive, decidedly English and fairly upper class."[53] Their fear derived in part from the possibility that large numbers of enthusiastic Sword members from outside the Church of Rome—for whom the ecumenical thrust of the new movement was its most attractive feature—would overwhelm the Roman Catholic members. Such an influx could cause the Sword to lose its original identity and focus, which was not ecumenism.[54] It could also lead to confusion when, under the auspices of the Sword, Protestant members made speeches and published articles that contained material at variance with Roman Catholic teaching.[55] Cardinal Hinsley pointed out that "we [Roman Catholics] cannot conceive the visible Church of Christ as merely a confederation of various Christian communities holding different and mutually exclusive doctrines. Such a union would not be a unity."[56] A Roman Catholic bishop remarked that

52. Purcell, *Fisher of Lambeth*, 106; Hastings, *History of English Christianity, 1920–2000*, 394–95; Jasper, *George Bell*, 249; Mews, "The Sword of the Spirit," 427; Walsh, "Ecumenism in War-Time Britain," 248.

53. Hastings, *History of English Christianity, 1920–2000*, 394.

54. Mews, "The Sword of the Spirit," 426–27. The Sword was not founded as an ecumenical venture. A chronicler of its early development writes that "it is hardly accurate to suggest that what would now be called ecumenism was in the minds of the founders of the movement, or indeed that it ever constituted a major part of its activities—though that is how Fr. Heenan, when a Cardinal, remembered it as he wrote his autobiography." Walsh, "Ecumenism in War-Time Britain (1)," 250.

55. Heenan, *Cardinal Hinsley*, 194.

56. Quoted in ibid., 196.

Anglicans and others might well ask how Roman Catholic clergy could be acting in concert with the local vicar while simultaneously "trying to persuade members of [the vicar's] congregation to believe he had no valid orders, and to leave his church."[57]

Although full membership in the Sword had to be restricted to Roman Catholics, sympathetic observers could set up a group that was parallel but distinct. Thus the Anglican and Free Church communions established an organization called Religion and Life. These two movements were then connected via a joint standing committee, designed to foster cooperation among all the churches that endorsed the principles of the Sword. Ably chaired by Geoffrey Fisher, this joint committee, with representatives from both Religion and Life and the Sword of the Spirit, held 17 meetings between 1942 and 1944. The bishop of London called the cooperation envisioned by the leaders of the movement "a measure of joint action such as has not happened in this country since the Reformation."[58]

Possessing the skills of a diplomat, Fisher was able to keep the representatives of the different religious bodies working together more or less effectively. Building upon enhanced cooperation and understanding among the various Christian communions, the joint committee hoped to advance a spiritual and social reformation in the world at large. After issuing a widely discussed Statement on Religious Co-operation in May 1942, however, the committee made little progress. Roman Catholics and Free Church members found themselves at loggerheads over a request from the latter for joint prayer, an activity that the Roman hierarchy was not yet ready for. A larger controversy arose over a proposed joint statement on religious freedom, an ecumenical development that the Roman Catholic authorities also concluded was a bridge too far.

Fisher was both saddened and annoyed by their response. In a confidential memorandum sent on September 14, 1944, to A. C. F. Beales, a Roman Catholic layman who carried out most of the administrative work for the Sword, Fisher said that Rome's rejection of the statement on religious freedom was "something worse than a disappointment." It raised a "fundamental question" concerning the Roman Catholic church's real reasons for refusing to go along.[59] At the September 18, 1944, meeting of the joint committee, Fisher asked whether Rome rejected the state-

57. W. F. Brown, "Cardinal Hinsley," 100. See the strongly critical response to the Roman Catholic policy in the *Church Times* lead article "Not Excalibur," August 15, 1941, quoted at length in Heeney, *Cardinal Hinsley*, 198–200.

58. Quoted in Iremonger, *William Temple, Archbishop of Canterbury*, 423.

59. Quoted in Walsh, "Ecumenism in War-Time Britain (2)," 391.

ment because it went beyond the proper work of the committee, because it improperly touched on matters of ecclesiastical doctrine, or because the statement's content was simply, from the Roman Catholic point of view, inexpedient, given the Church of Rome's desire to safeguard its position in Roman Catholic countries.[60] In fact, the entire movement had been dealt a crippling blow in March 1943, when its leading light, Cardinal Hinsley, died.[61]

He was succeeded at Westminster by Archbishop Bernard Griffin, who was, Hastings notes, "a great deal more circumspect." Under him, "the Sword would shrink till it became little more than a penknife."[62] Thus, Geoffrey Fisher later lamented, "the whole thing sank, without any result. That was a great disappointment."[63]

For Fisher, however, chairing the joint committee was in important respects a valuable experience, a preparation for what lay ahead. For the first time he had undertaken a task that brought him into close and lively contact with outstanding Roman Catholic thinkers.[64] Like his efforts to bring about clerical discipline in the diocese of London, this work would end in disappointment—but not in disillusionment. As archbishop of Canterbury, he would have another chance—a larger opportunity—to effect change in the areas of both ecclesiastical order and ecumenical relations. As archbishop he would also have to focus considerable attention on the role of the church in the nation and in the world community.

60. Ibid. Walsh writes: "Fisher could not have been far from the truth when he wrote, in his memorandum for the meeting of 18 September 1944: 'The Roman Catholic authorities may feel that while the document correctly expresses the principles of natural justice and does not directly conflict with their principles of ecclesiastical doctrine, yet, owing to the conditions of their own Church in various countries, its publication would be inexpedient and place them in difficulty'—which comes close to accusing Roman Catholics of having double standards." Walsh, "Ecumenism in War-Time (2)," 392.

61. Purcell, *Fisher of Lambeth*, 106–7; *ODCC*, 3d ed., s.v. "Sword of the Spirit"; Jasper, *George Bell*, 251–53; Carpenter, *Archbishop Fisher*, 104–109; Walsh, "Ecumenism in War-Time (1)," 255–58.

62. Hastings, *History of English Christianity, 1920–2000*, 396.

63. Quoted in Purcell, *Fisher of Lambeth*, 107. Jasper provides a broader view and a more positive reading of the fruits of these joint endeavors in his *George Bell*, 254–55. See also Carpenter, *Archbishop Fisher*, 113–14.

64. Carpenter, *Archbishop Fisher*, 113.

3

Archbishop of Canterbury, 1945–1961

The Church of England

The Death of Archbishop William Temple

O N October 26, 1944, at the age of sixty-three, William Temple died unexpectedly. The spiritual leader of the Anglican Communion for but a short time—a mere two and a half years—he has since been reckoned one of the greatest men ever to have occupied the Chair of St. Augustine of Canterbury. When someone asked the Conservative prime minister why he had appointed a socialist to this most important see, Winston Churchill famously replied that Temple was "the only sixpenny article in a penny bazaar."[1] Geoffrey Fisher was in the Bishops' Robing Room of the House of Lords when he received the news of Temple's death. "I knelt down at one of the chairs," he recalled, "and . . . I was there for about an hour not thinking about anything at all but just trying to assimilate myself to a completely changed world and a completely changed Church."[2]

It would be good to know what each of these figures thought of the other man. What distinguished them from one another would have been obvious to both, and from early on. As his immediate successor at Repton School, Fisher would have been deeply aware of Temple's strengths and weaknesses as a leader, a scholar, and a person; and over the years Temple would have grown increasingly familiar with Fisher's skills and deficien-

1. Quoted in Edwards, *Leaders of the Church of England, 1828–1978*, 353. In his diary, Sir Alexander Cadogan, the secretary of the Cabinet during the war years, recorded Churchill's reaction to Temple's death: "Thursday, 26 October 1944. News came of death of Archbishop of Canterbury. P.M. delighted." Quoted in Beeson, *The Church of England in Crisis*, 101.

2. Quoted in Carpenter, *Archbishop Fisher*, 129.

cies. Their similarities would also have been apparent to both men: their educational and religious backgrounds, their outstanding intellects, their support of ecumenism, and their reliability as high-ranking officials of the church. In their different ways, both men were ecclesiastical thorough-breds, capable of meeting tough challenges without flinching. Each had an unwavering commitment to the good of the Church of England. They undoubtedly felt a large measure of affection and respect for one another.

Six years younger than William Temple, Geoffrey Fisher was neither his predecessor's peer nor his protégé, still less his underling. And yet many times as bishop of London he helped out the archbishop in the Upper House of the Convocation of Canterbury by taking care of the business that Temple did not like to handle. Fisher provided some insights into their working relationship when he said that

> Lang had dominated [the House of Bishops] too much, and William Temple was a very different kind of person. He was per-fectly clear on principles, but he was not really interested in the process of reducing principles to rules or regulations or clear direc-tion. As it happened, I had always had an interest in this kind of process, and a good deal of experience in it. I think William appre-ciated and valued that fact and it enabled me to take some things off him. As Bishop of London, under him, I made it my duty to keep an eye upon the details of many matters, to see how con-flicting details might be brought to order, and irreconcilable views brought together. It was work which exactly suited me. William Temple, meanwhile, living on a higher level, spiritually and intel-lectually, could draw people together in seeking and finding some-times a statement by a mere verbal alteration in a resolution which could be accepted as the right conclusion in accordance with the will of God.[3]

The relationship between these two churchmen was like that of elder to younger brother, where two gifted siblings acknowledge one another's dif-fering skills and interests but each brother also recognizes—with apprecia-tion undiluted by rivalry—the other's brilliance and utter devotion to the family firm. At the very least, Temple and Fisher must have seen their respective talents as strongly complementary.[4]

3. Quoted in Purcell, *Fisher of Lambeth*, 98.
4. In the late 1950s, Peter Kirk, the son of Bishop K. E. Kirk, commented that Fisher's "basic virtue is his great business acumen, something in which Temple was completely lacking. They would have made a great team together, as in many ways they were comple-mentary." Kirk, *One Army Strong?*, 71.

Winston Churchill would take two months to decide who should be the next archbishop of Canterbury. Not long before he died, William Temple, enjoying his last summer holiday with his wife and talking with her about retirement, indicated that he thought the choice an obvious one: "I must give up in time to let Geoffrey have his whack."[5]

Churchill's Choice

Among all the bishops and archbishops in the Anglican Communion, the archbishop of Canterbury had a uniquely complex role to play. Besides being bishop of the diocese of Canterbury (which consisted of the county of Kent east of the river Medway together with the rural deanery of Croydon), he had jurisdiction over all 29 dioceses in the southern province of the Church of England. Thus he presided over the Upper House of the Convocation of Canterbury, as well as over the Church Assembly. Like other senior bishops, the archbishop of Canterbury was a member of the House of Lords. He alone crowned the British monarch. Because the archbishop of Canterbury was also the spiritual leader of the worldwide Anglican Communion, he presided over the Lambeth Conference, the decennial gathering of Anglican bishops.

As early as 1942, following the retirement of Cosmo Lang, some members of the Conservative Party, impressed with Fisher's performance as bishop of London, recommended him to Churchill as an alternative to William Temple. These Conservatives were troubled by the prospect of a Temple primacy, for the archbishop of York was a highly engaging man of the Left.[6] On this occasion, the premier did not choose Fisher, presumably because he did not deem his worth to be appreciably superior to that of the other articles in the penny bazaar. But after Temple's death Fisher emerged as the leading candidate to succeed him, although two other English bishops were also in the running: Cyril Garbett, who had succeeded Temple at York, and George Bell, the longtime bishop of Chichester.[7]

An impressive man—diligent, commonsensical, and widely respected—Garbett had just one drawback: his age. Before his translation to York he had been bishop of Southwark, where he oversaw the beginning of religious broadcasting, and then bishop of Winchester, where he also proved

5. Quoted in Iremonger, *William Temple, Archbishop of Canterbury,* 620.

6. Palmer, *A Class of Their Own,* 186; Smyth, *Cyril Forster Garbett,* 274.

7. Another candidate seriously considered by Churchill was Mervyn Haigh, the bishop of Winchester. See Palmer, *High and Mitred,* 225; and Barry, *Mervyn Haigh,* 191. Palmer notes, however, that Haigh was unhealthy, highly strung, and indecisive.

himself an able pastor and an effective teacher.[8] He believed, however, that he was too old to take up this new work: "I should be at least 73 by the next Lambeth Conference and ought to resign at 75." He also felt that he lacked "the gifts for this post," although many would have disagreed with his assessment. In Garbett's view, Canterbury needed a dynamic presence for some years, not a caretaker, and Geoffrey Fisher fit the bill: "I should work with him with great happiness."[9]

At 63, George Bell was young enough to be an effective archbishop, and he knew Lambeth Palace inside and out. While in his thirties he had served as secretary to Randall Davidson (archbishop of Canterbury from 1903 to 1928), and he had been assistant secretary to the 1920 Lambeth Conference. In 1935 he published a well-executed, two-volume biography of Davidson. As dean of Canterbury (1924–29), he abolished visitors' fees and arranged for the first performance of religious drama in an English cathedral in modern times (John Masefield's *The Coming of Christ*). As bishop of Chichester, he was both a thoughtful innovator in his own diocese, encouraging religious education and religious art, and an excellent pastor and administrator. He was also a major figure in the church at large. Indeed, after William Temple, Bell was the most highly regarded Anglican in the international religious community. For many years a leader of the ecumenical movement, he supported the Confessing Church in its opposition to the Nazi regime, and he established important contacts with German Christians, including the Lutheran pastor Dietrich Bonhoeffer, hanged by the Gestapo at Flossenbürg in 1945.[10]

But, like Cyril Garbett, Bell had an Achilles' heel, at least as far as Churchill was concerned. He had made speeches criticizing the government's war policy. On February 9, 1944, the bishop of Chichester delivered a widely reported speech in the House of Lords questioning the morality of the strategic bombing offensive against German cities: "I desire to challenge the Government on the policy which directs the bombing of enemy towns on the present scale, especially with reference to civilians who are non-combatants, and non-military and non-industrial objectives." Bell's challenge was based on traditional just-war theory, which prohibits the intentional killing of non-combatants. He asked whether the government was aware of the moral implications of its actions or of the harm that its policies would do to future relations with the peoples of Europe. "The

8. Edwards, *Leaders*, 354.

9. Quoted in Smyth, *Cyril Forster Garbett*, 295.

10. Edwards, *Leaders*, 354–55.

policy," he declared, "is obliteration, openly acknowledged. That is not a justifiable act of war." And then he added this statement, which dared to suggest a moral equivalence in Allied and Axis war methods as well as in their justification: "To justify attacks inhuman in themselves by arguments of expediency smacks of the Nazi philosophy that Might is Right."[11]

This speech undoubtedly hurt Bell's chances to be archbishop, though it was not the only factor. A shy man who was uncomfortable with small talk, he had an unfortunate reputation—though no reader would guess it from the speech just quoted—as a dull speaker, given to lecturing his audience. And he could be a mulish opponent.[12] In any case, Churchill chose Fisher, and once again Bell suffered being passed over for higher preferment. As one twentieth-century church historian has observed, however, "[b]eing the senior clergyman in Sussex cannot be martyrdom."[13]

From Churchill's comment about "the only sixpenny article," we have a good idea of what the premier thought of William Temple. But we know little about Churchill's assessment of Geoffrey Fisher, whose social and political outlook he would have found more congenial than either Temple's or Bell's. The premier must have been aware of Fisher's reputation as a skilled executive, and we can be sure that he would have heard from his advisors that what the Church of England needed in the postwar era was not a prophetic figure but a top-flight administrator who would modernize the church's organization and finances.[14]

A student of history would have enjoyed being invisibly present in No. 10 Downing Street when, during his luncheon interview with Fisher, the prime minister asked the bishop of London what he thought of a rationalistic exercise titled *Vie de Jésus*. Written by the French historian and philosopher Ernest Renan, this popular work—it sold 60,000 copies in its first six months—presents Jesus as an amiable Galilean preacher: a sublime human being but not a divine personage. The *Vie de Jésus* caused a sensation when it was published in 1863, and it led to Renan's removal from his appointment as a professor of Hebrew at the Collège de France.[15]

Churchill would have been more in sympathy with the skeptical tenor of this book than Fisher would have been, for the prime minister

11. Bell, *The Church and Humanity,* 129–41; Jasper, *George Bell,* 284–85; Hein, "George Bell, Bishop of Chichester, on the Morality of War"; Staples, "Archbishop Geoffrey Francis Fisher: An Appraisal," 246–47; Edwards, *Leaders,* 357.

12. Edwards, *Leaders,* 355–56; Jasper, *George Bell,* 285–86; Palmer, *High and Mitred,* 226.

13. Edwards, *Leaders,* 358.

14. Beeson, *The Bishops,* 128.

15. *ODCC,* 3rd ed., s.v. "Renan, Joseph Ernest."

did not care for either Christian theology or church officials.[16] Once, during an after-dinner speech when he was archbishop of Canterbury, Fisher referred to Churchill, who was present, as a source of great support in certain ecclesiastical matters. Churchill replied, "I hope that, when you call me a supporter of the Church, you do not imply that I am a *pillar* of the Church. I am not. Though I might perhaps claim to be a buttress—a flying buttress, on the outside."[17] On the occasion of his Downing Street interview, Fisher admitted to the prime minister that he had never read Renan's *Vie de Jésus*. "What, you've never read it!" he later recalled Churchill exclaiming.[18] And there, presumably, the subject was dropped, with Geoffrey Fisher letting pass an opportunity for a searching colloquy on approaches to the historical Jesus.

After what some observers—including Archbishop Garbett—thought an indecent interval, Winston Churchill, busy with the Pacific campaign and frankly lacking either interest in or knowledge of ecclesiastical appointments, chose Geoffrey Fisher to be the 99th archbishop of Canterbury.[19] The appointment was announced on January 2, 1945. At the time of his selection, Fisher was known in his own diocese but not well known throughout the country. As one historian has said of him, "he did not emerge at the end of the Second World War as a truly national figure." Much better known were both Archbishop Garbett, "a solid and ever-dependable national figure," and the "controversial" George Bell. Also, of course, the new archbishop "was not cast in the same mould as the sublimely charismatic Temple."[20]

He was simply Geoffrey Fisher: eager to modernize the functioning of the Church of England, to build up the Anglican Communion, and to reach out in ecumenical friendship to other Christian bodies. Which is not to say that he coveted the post of archbishop of Canterbury, for he had grown to like his London diocese very much. By the time he left, he had visited fully half of its 600 parishes. Feeling that he was especially capable in the role of committee chairman, moving disparate personalities toward a positive result, he knew that the one episcopal task he particu-

16. Edwards, *Leaders*, 353.

17. *Church Times*, January 29, 1965, 15. The author of this *Church Times* article said that this story was "supplied by the Rev. P. N. H. Coney, of Milverton, Taunton, . . . [who] had it from Archbishop Garbett in 1952." Another version of this story appears in Horne, *Harold Macmillan: 1957–1986*, 611.

18. GF, quoted in Purcell, *Fisher of Lambeth*, 110.

19. Smyth, *Cyril Forster Garbett*, 296.

20. Staples, "Archbishop Geoffrey Francis Fisher," 242–43.

larly disliked was a duty that he would have to perform over and over again as Cantuar: "The one thing I did not like," he recalled, "was pronouncements, the sort of thing one has to say on one's own authority, as one's own final judgment. . . . I said [to Cyril Garbett] I couldn't face that. . . ."[21] But in the end, of course, he said yes when the archbishopric was offered, and he came to this conclusion without the perturbation that accompanied his decision to go to London. And, in time, his reluctance to issue public pronouncements gave way to a far greater willingness to make himself heard on the day's controversies. Indeed, "[d]uring his Canterbury years," writes one episcopal historian, "he could not keep quiet."[22]

How did those who knew him well regard his selection? Archbishop Garbett's diary comment may be fairly representative: Fisher "has not Temple's genius, but he has great ability, especially on the administrative side, combined with charm and humility."[23] But those who thought that the postwar church needed a prophet were undoubtedly disappointed.[24]

On April 19, 1945, as the Second World War was entering its final months, Geoffrey Fisher was enthroned in Canterbury Cathedral as Primate of All England. Less than three weeks later, on May 9, the Allies celebrated V-E (Victory-in-Europe) Day. On August 14, following the devastation of Hiroshima and Nagasaki by atomic blasts, Imperial Japan surrendered.

Fisher's primacy began with the commencement of the atomic age, the beginning of the Cold War, and the continuation of deprivation and anxiety. A visitor in the early 1950s found England to be "a cold, bleak, bombed-out, seedy, unpainted, half-lit place, a country of rationing and austerity that appeared to be recovering much more slowly from the traumas of the war than . . . Italy and France. . . ."[25] The Fishers' own home in London, Lambeth Palace, substantially rebuilt around 1830, had been heavily damaged by bombing. In 1945, at the end of the war, the thirteenth-century chapel stood completely gutted, and the Great Hall was still partly roofless. Restoration of the palace proved to be an extensive and prolonged operation, lasting from 1945 to 1955.[26]

21. Quoted in Purcell, *Fisher of Lambeth*, 108.

22. Beeson, *The Bishops*, 131.

23. Quoted in Smyth, *Cyril Forster Garbett*, 295.

24. Palmer, *High and Mitred*, 225.

25. Jacobson, "'If England Was What England Seems.'" See Tony Judt, *Postwar*, 162–63; Dominic Sandbrook, *Never Had It So Good*, 44–45; and Wilson, *After the Victorians*, 518.

26. Purcell, *Fisher of Lambeth*, 129–35. Charles Smyth writes that GF, "as Archbishop of Canterbury, amid all the labours of preparing for the Lambeth Conference of 1948, . . .

The new archbishop would have to face both the material wreck-age and the spiritual unease so ably depicted by Rose Macaulay in *The World My Wilderness*. Confronting the desolate areas of cities and souls, he would have to do what he could to fix, in her words, "the roofless, gaping churches," the bombed-out shells that "gaped like lost myths."[27] He would not only have to carry out routine maintenance but also build for the future, and for that he would need a vision.

Geoffrey Fisher's strategic plan encompassed two major goals: First, to improve the administration, finances, and laws of the church so that the pastoral ministry could be carried out more effectively. Second, to fortify the Church Universal by strengthening the ties both among worldwide Anglicans and among the various Christian communions—Protestant, Roman Catholic, and Orthodox.[28] "Strengthen," in this case, did not usually mean "tighten." Better relations grew out of open communica-tion, mutual respect, and in some cases a loosening of bonds. Note that Fisher's goals did not include remaking theology, deepening spirituality, or altering the church-state relationship. Because he accepted the underlying structures of church and society as givens, he may best be characterized as a conservative reformer.

Reforming Canon Law

It is fitting that our review of the archiepiscopate of Geoffrey Fisher should begin with his superintendence of the Church of England, for he regarded the internal administration of the church as his primary responsibility. And, although it may seem strange to us today, he believed, looking back on his career, that revision of the canons—the laws by which the church governs itself—was his greatest achievement.

The canons in effect when Fisher took office were still those of 1604, which were issued by King James VI and I just after the death of Queen Elizabeth I. Some of these laws—for example, rules about clergy night-

enjoyed chatting naturally, as man to man, with the workmen who were restoring Lambeth Palace. . . , and one of his former Chaplains writes: 'I think he knew more about their families by the time their work was finished than . . . their employers did.' . . . Nor was it necessary for Geoffrey Fisher, as it was for William Temple, to try to come down to their level, because, from his broader experience of life, he had a genius for getting quickly and effortlessly onto easy terms with anyone that he met, simply by being his natural, friendly self." Smyth, "In Duty's Path: Fisher of Lambeth," 68.

27. Macaulay, *The World My Wilderness*, 61, 254.
28. Lloyd, *The Church of England, 1900–1965*, 466.

caps and the wearing of yellow stockings—were completely out of date.[29] Some of them—such as proper vestments for morning prayer—were still obeyed.[30] Others were openly flouted. Too often the lack of a modern code had caused not tolerance and harmony but dissension, as the various church parties took advantage of the dearth of clear guidelines. "Many of the conflicts which engaged the Victorian and post-Victorian bishops," David L. Edwards points out, "arose because the Church of England had ceased to have an acceptable and enforceable code of regulations."[31] In the absence of up-to-date rules, each bishop had tried to act as the legal authority in his diocese, with the archbishop of Canterbury playing an appellate role. But, as Edwards notes, "the situation was a nightmare to anyone with an orderly mind."[32] To some extent, the movement for reform of the canons was driven by laypeople. "The later developments of the Oxford Movement had plunged the Church of England into a condition approaching liturgical anarchy," another historian, Charles Smyth, has noted, "and for nearly a century the laity had been indignantly demanding that the bishops should put their house in order."[33]

Fisher was not, of course, the first person to recognize the need to resolve this problem. Archbishops Cosmo Lang and William Temple had set up the Canon Law Commission in 1939. Chaired by Archbishop Garbett, who succeeded Temple at York, this commission issued a report in 1947, *The Canon Law of the Church of England*, which made it clear that canon-law revision was required. This report provided a historical introduction to canon law and proposed a set of 134 canons.[34] Reform was necessary, but whether the canons had to come up in the way they did under Fisher, year after year, like the chancery case in *Bleak House*, is another question. Not until 1969 was the new body of canon law finally approved.

In a larger sense, however, canon-law reform may be taken as but a part for the whole. What Fisher was really after was a transformation of the Church of England so that it could meet the demands of a changed and rapidly changing world. He sought to rebuild the church in order to render it capable of ministering to a modern, postwar society. And updating the canons was a necessary though clearly not a sufficient step in this

29. Chadwick, *Michael Ramsey*, 101.

30. Ibid.

31. Edwards, *Leaders*, 360.

32. Ibid.

33. Smyth, "In Duty's Path," 70.

34. Moorman, *A History of the Church in England*, 440.

effort of reconstruction. Whether it should have been a central focus of Fisher's and the church's attention all during these crucial postwar years is a question that is still debated.

To Fisher canon-law revision did lie at the heart of what was needed. He later referred to this work as "the most absorbing and all-embracing topic of my archiepiscopate."[35] This former headmaster had a high view of the law. "[T]he clergy," he said, "ought to be bound by canons; that [is] what canonical obedience means." When canons are breached, "[c]onsistory courts ought to be able to impose penalties, even deprivation."[36] In this strict attitude toward canon law he differed from his predecessor, for William Temple distinguished between obeying a canon "with mechanical uniformity" and observing it "with reverent regard." A canon, Temple said, ought to be "followed with that freedom of spontaneity which belongs to the spiritual life" that the canon itself was designed to regulate. "Nothing could more conduce to the true welfare of our Church than a recovery of the original sense of canonical authority as something which claims not detailed conformity but reverent loyalty."[37] Temple's approach—focusing on "loyalty"—allowed greater freedom of interpretation than Fisher's more black-or-white, legalistic understanding.[38] In his strict attitude toward canon law Fisher also differed from his successor, Michael Ramsey, an Anglo-Catholic. While not in favor of anarchy, Ramsey disliked the idea of using law to impose conformity on worship.[39]

Both Anglo-Catholics and evangelical Anglicans were apprehensive about the possible results of canon-law revision. In 1957, for example, a small group of evangelical leaders, including John Stott, the rector of All Souls, Langham Place, London, called on Geoffrey Fisher at Lambeth Palace to let him know what concerned them about the revisions. By this time, as Stott's biographer writes, revision was "dragging its slow length along on the floor of the Church Assembly."[40] The process was now in its eleventh year. Doubting that the new canons would effect any positive change in what the evangelicals cared most about—evangelism, personal holiness, and vital worship—these evangelical leaders worried that the result might be to impose on them liturgical requirements that were, in

35. Quoted in Edwards, *Leaders*, 360.
36. Quoted in Carpenter, *Archbishop Fisher*, 209.
37. William Temple, foreword to Bullard, *Standing Orders of the Church of England*, vi.
38. Dudley-Smith, *John Stott*, 310.
39. Chadwick, *Michael Ramsey*, 101.
40. Dudley-Smith, *John Stott*, 309.

their eyes, theologically unacceptable. If—to cite a principal concern—the revised canon law required them to wear eucharistic vestments, such as chasubles, then this apparel might imply their endorsement of the Roman view of the Mass—of priesthood, sacrifice, even transubstantiation. These understandings of the Lord's Supper were inconsistent with the reformed interpretation not only of the Holy Communion but also of the life of faith in response to the work of Christ. Or, if the canons said that only communicant members of the Anglican church could receive Holy Communion, then evangelical Anglican clergy would be required to drop their practice of the "open table," according to which communicant members of other denominations were admitted to the Lord's Supper. At All Souls, for example, John Stott always invited, as he put it, "any baptized and communicant member of another church who loves and trusts the Lord Jesus" to receive the consecrated bread and wine.[41]

At the same time, Anglo-Catholics feared the imposition of restrictions on liturgical customs that they had long practiced. Ritualists, Fisher's obituarist in *The Times* recalled, worried that Cantuar's aim was to allow, "under the guise of liberalism, certain modest deviations from the Book of Common Prayer merely in order to get an excuse for enforcing conformity more vigorously than before." They feared that in "the name of the middle way . . . he was plotting the destruction of the Anglo-Catholic movement as a prelude to the creation of an unequivocally Protestant National Church," which would then be absorbed "in a loose federation of Churches without even the common bond of episcopacy."[42] Meanwhile, Anglican liberals, most anxious about how the laws would be enforced, feared the outbreak of wholesale prosecutions for disobedience.[43]

Notwithstanding these inevitable anxieties, the revision of canon law went forward, with Fisher providing generally effective guidance of the Convocations as well as of the House of Laity in the Church Assembly. The different church parties could see, from the legislation taking shape, that when the process was completed the church would be both comprehensive and more prescriptive. In the matter of clerical vestments, for example, the canons would not prescribe only one mode of attire but rather an acceptable range of options.[44] The debates over canon-law revision led, Fisher said later, to "major clashes" and to "dismay and discouragement"

41. Ibid., 310.

42. "Lord Fisher of Lambeth, Former Archbishop of Canterbury," *The Times*, September 16, 1972.

43. Ibid.

44. Edwards, *Leaders*, 360–61.

caused by the expenditure of so much time and energy on a "seemingly endless task." Cantuar sometimes had to exert himself to keep his teams in harness: "More than once, to the bishops or in Church Assembly, I had to hold forth at length about the central place of canon law for the renewal of the Church."[45]

The process was often unwieldy. One aspect of canon-law revision—overhauling the ecclesiastical courts—meant repealing or amending 200 acts of Parliament. Transforming this system of church courts proved so large and complex a task that it had to be spun off from the work of canon revision and handed to another commission to take on. In a debate in the Church Assembly, Geoffrey Fisher argued for retaining the judicial committee of the Privy Council as the final court of appeal in ecclesiastical cases. But his opinion flew directly in the face of the expressed views of most members of the Church Assembly. Why, they asked, should the judicial committee of the Privy Council, which is a court of laymen appointed by the state, decide questions of worship and doctrine?[46] It was during this debate that members of the Assembly shouted "No!" at the archbishop of Canterbury.[47]

Many were unhappy with either the process or the results of canon-law revision. W. R. Matthews, the former dean of St. Paul's Cathedral in London, may be representative of those who held an alternative—perhaps more Temple-like—view of how canon-law reform should have been carried out. Matthews thought that taking the "detailed legislation of 1604 . . . as a model for 1950" was "a fatal mistake." He believed that the only discipline needed was "a set of principles laying down in a broad way the purposes and ideals of the pastoral office, as understood in the Anglican branch of the Catholic Church." The bishops should be fathers in God to their clergy, encouraging and helping them. Instead, the revised canons made the bishops too much the authority figures. Matthews noted that the language of the canons reflected this stress on hierarchy: "Reading through them, one constantly comes upon 'with the consent of the bishop' or 'shall

---

45. Quoted in Edwards, *Leaders*, 361.

46. Welsby, *A History of the Church of England, 1945–1980*, 43.

47. Kemp, "Chairmanly Cantuar," 23. See also Kemp's comments on the impetus that canon-law revision gave to other important matters that had to be dealt with separately, including the role of the laity in church government and the revision of liturgical rites. The situation related to church courts was more complicated than indicated here; on the problems and inutility of the judicial committee, see Welsby, *History of the Church of England*, 43.

be referred to the bishop,' all expressions tending to restrict the initiative of the parish priest."[48]

Others viewed the amount of work involved as effort that would have been better expended elsewhere. After describing the tortuous path that each canon had to take before winning final approval, one observer wryly noted that when the process was finally completed, members of the Church of England learned that a man was not allowed to marry his daughter, that the clergy should prepare for confirmation persons who wished to be confirmed, that every church should have a copy of the prayer book, and that clergy should wear suitable attire.[49]

The Bishop Barnes Affair

The canons aimed at the discipline of the whole church. In the Bishop Barnes affair, Archbishop Fisher faced a situation involving the discipline of one person, and no laws could tell him precisely how to handle this problem. In retrospect, we can see that the most interesting aspects of this case had to do not so much with Bishop Barnes and his controversial book, which was not a significant scholarly achievement, as with other aspects of the problem: The conundrum presented by Bishop Barnes was both an administrator's nightmare and a harbinger of things to come.

Although he was trained in mathematics and was not a biblical scholar, the bishop of Birmingham, Ernest William Barnes, undertook to write a book about the origins of the Christian religion. Published in 1947, *The Rise of Christianity* caused a stir because it was so frankly dismissive of traditional Christian dogma, especially the miraculous. In this book, for example, Barnes calls the birth stories "edifying legend."[50] He observes that the roots of the story of the Virgin Birth are "pagan."[51] He questions the doctrine of the Logos—the eternal Word incarnate in this man, Jesus—set forth in the first chapter of John's Gospel.[52] And he denies the bodily resurrection of Christ.[53] Like Thomas Jefferson, he admires Jesus' character and teaching.[54] If Barnes had been a professor at Oxford or Cambridge, these claims would scarcely have raised an eyebrow. The difficulty was that

48. Matthews, *Memories and Meanings*, 306.

49. Beeson, *The Church of England in Crisis*, 124.

50. Barnes, *The Rise of Christianity*, 68.

51. Ibid., 87.

52. Ibid., 97.

53. Ibid., 166, 170.

54. Welsby, *History of the Church of England*, 54.

a sitting Anglican bishop was making them, a person charged with teaching others the historic Christian faith. Unlike many mediocre works of non-fiction, this book did not die aborning. It was widely noticed, and it caused a commotion. How should an archbishop respond?

Fisher found that Barnes had strayed too far from orthodoxy in his statements touching on the Incarnation and the Resurrection. In a private letter the archbishop told him: "You make fundamental departures from the doctrines held by the communion to which you belong." He stated that "the holding of your opinions and the holding of your office are incompatible, and for myself I believe that you ought in conscience to feel the same."[55] In his reply Barnes pointed out that his book was an attempt to depict the early history of Christianity, not to write Anglican theology; moreover, he did not believe that his views were incompatible with church teachings.[56]

Under increasing pressure to take action, the archbishop of Canterbury had to choose one of three options: ignore the book, arraign its author on heresy charges, or do something in between these extremes (a public statement of condemnation or disavowal?). The case for ignoring the book was strong. The highly respected theologian Leonard Hodgson, Regius Professor of Divinity at Oxford, came up with what may have been the best alternative: Balance doing nothing with offering a positive statement, a clear affirmation by the bishops of the central tenets of the Christian faith. Bishops William Wand of London and K. E. Kirk of Oxford also advocated a policy of benign neglect.[57] In practical terms, a quiet approach stood the best chance of curtailing additional publicity and sales for the book, which had not received glowing reviews. But other bishops, including Cyril Garbett, urged Fisher to take a stand in opposition to Barnes, though no one was pushing for a heresy trial.[58] Even a debate in Convocation, Cantuar realized, would be impossible to keep within foreseeable bounds, and therefore should be avoided.[59]

Fisher decided that he had to say something publicly, and so he opted for a straightforward statement in the full synod of the Convocation of Canterbury. Dean Matthews recalled that "[t]he Archbishop was confronted by a majority of bishops who would have insisted on passing a

55. Barnes, *Ahead of His Age,* 405.

56. Ibid.

57. Carpenter, *Archbishop Fisher,* 297.

58. Barnes, *Ahead of His Age,* 406.

59. Ibid., 408.

vote of censure for heresy unless he spoke plainly condemning Barnes's theology and he chose the course which was least provocative."[60]

In his President's Address, delivered at a joint meeting of both houses on October 15, 1947, Fisher noted that *The Rise of Christianity* had caused "both distress and indignation among Church people." In this book, Cantuar declared, Bishop Barnes "discards or omits . . . much which holds a central place in generally accepted Christian doctrine and belief." Indeed, his book "so diminishes . . . the content of the Christian Faith as to make the residue which is left inconsistent with the scriptural doctrine and beliefs of the Church in which [Barnes] holds office." For example, the bishop of Birmingham "reduces the resurrection of Our Lord to a subjective conviction on the part of His disciples." A book containing such an inadequate expression of the church's doctrine "cannot but disturb and shock us." A bishop has "stricter standards" applied to him. In his teaching he must "adequately and faithfully" express "the general doctrines of the Church and their scriptural basis which he is pledged by his office to defend and promote." Barnes may be convinced that his book is in accord with church teaching, but "I must say . . . that I am not so satisfied. If his views were mine, I should not feel that I could still hold episcopal office in the Church."[61]

Bishop Barnes defended his work and refused to resign.[62] No further official action was taken against him. On his subsequent visits to the diocese of Birmingham, however, Fisher shunned Barnes, turning down his offers of hospitality. Cantuar believed that to visit the bishop would imply some kind of endorsement and thereby undermine the point of his statement in Convocation. In his account of the archbishop's treatment of the bishop of Birmingham, John Barnes (the bishop's son) reminds his readers of Cantuar's former career: "As the headmaster could not sack his wayward housemaster, he preferred to ignore him and deal directly with the prefects."[63]

Barnes's refusal to retract his controversial statements coupled with Geoffrey Fisher's disinclination to opt for more-punitive measures against the bishop of Birmingham reflected and reinforced those features of the Anglican ethos which favored breadth and toleration. As Laurie, the central character in *The Towers of Trebizond*, observes, "Anglicans have less

60. Matthews, *Memories and Meanings*, 310.

61. *Chronicle of Convocation, 1947*, 187, 188, 190, 191.

62. Barnes, *Ahead of His Age*, 412.

63. Ibid., 418.

certainty but more scope, and can use their imaginations more."[64] The outcome of the Barnes case tended to affirm Anglicans' (even bishops') freedom to accept radical biblical criticism and modernist interpretations of Christian doctrine.[65] Of course the way that bishops made use of their freedom would continue to give headaches to the hierarchy of the Church of England. The Barnes case anticipated the challenge that Archbishop Michael Ramsey faced 16 years later when John A. T. Robinson, the suffragan bishop of Woolwich, published *Honest to God*.

Fisher had his own run-in with Bishop Robinson in 1960 when Robinson appeared for the publishers (Penguin Books) in the obscenity trial concerning an unexpurgated version of D. H. Lawrence's *Lady Chatterley's Lover*. In his responses in court Robinson went so far as to say that the novel "portrays the life of a woman in an immoral relationship, in so far as adultery is an immoral relationship." Asked if Lawrence's novel was a book that Christians ought to read, Robinson replied, "Yes, I think it is."[66]

A few days after the trial, Fisher sent Robinson a letter in which he reminded him that he had given the bishop "a private hint which you did not welcome. I am now in the very embarrassing position of having to answer protests of distressed and indignant people at the evidence which you gave. . . ." He told Robinson, "I cannot defend you, of course, at all." Because "the distress which you have caused to very many Christian people is so great . . . I think I must say something in public." He enclosed a copy of the brief statement he proposed to make: "I was preparing to say a good deal more, but in the end I made it as brief as I could without obscuring what I had to say."[67]

Two days later, on November 5, 1960, Fisher publicly rebuked Robinson at the diocesan conference at Canterbury. He took Robinson

64. Macaulay, *The Towers of Trebizond*, 203.

65. Snape, "A Dean and an Archbishop," 289. See Raven, "E.W.B.—The Man for the Moment."

66. GF Papers 246, fols. 158–59. Robinson's comments are from a newspaper cutting appended to a letter from the Reverend L. H. Cuckney, of Wimbledon, to Col. R. J. A. Hornby, Chief Information Officer, Church House, Westminster, October 29, 1960, in which Cuckney refers to the trial and to the effect it might have on parishioners. See Machin, *Churches and Social Issues in Twentieth-Century Britain*, 187; Robinson, *Christian Freedom in a Permissive Society*, chap. 4, "Obscenity and Maturity"; and James, *A Life of Bishop John A. T. Robinson*, 93–96. James points out that most people in the court interpreted Robinson's words "in so far as adultery is an immoral relationship" to mean "inasmuch as adultery" is immoral (95).

67. GF to Robinson, November 3, 1960, GF Papers 246, fol. 160.

to task for supposing that he could give testimony in this trial and not be "a stumbling-block and a cause of offence to many ordinary Christians." Fisher declared, "The Christian fact is that adultery . . . is always a sin, and . . . at present a very prominent, even all pervasive, one. The good pastor will teach his people to avoid both the fact of and the desire for sex experience of an adulterous kind. . . ."[68]

The Church Commissioners

When he was bishop of London, Geoffrey Fisher began work to reorganize the finances of the Church of England. Often the fact that he was not a spiritual adept or a theologian or an academic proved to be just as well for the rank-and-file clergy. Like many other sons of the vicarage, he knew the church, and therefore he was not a churchy person. He had a practical common sense and an empathy rooted in experience which could work to the advantage of the clerical soldiers in the field. As we have already seen, when Fisher was headmaster of Repton, he could handle a welter of details in an efficient manner while holding in mind the larger strategic plan. At the end of the Second World War, his strategic plan for the Church of England incorporated, as one of its chief goals, improving the abysmal stipends of parish clergy.

In order to increase the remuneration of clergy, Fisher knew that he had to raise revenues. The best chance of accomplishing this objective lay in consolidating the financial agencies of the church and focusing on greater investment productivity. To these ends, in 1948 he oversaw the amalgamation of the Ecclesiastical Commissioners and Queen Anne's Bounty to form a new agency called the Church Commissioners for England. Established as a permanent body in 1836, the Ecclesiastical Commissioners had been the main trustees of the church's endowments, the earnings from which were used to augment the endowment income of the poorer benefices. A smaller agency, Queen Anne's Bounty, established in 1704, used its funds to help support underpaid clergy and to provide funds to repair clergy houses, but by 1945 the financial assistance that it was providing to parishes was meager.[69] The most important function of the new, combined body, the Church Commissioners, was to hold, invest, and administer the endowments of the Church of England. If their invest-

---

68. GF Papers 246, fol. 162. See *The Times*, November 7, 1960; Machin, *Churches and Social Issues*, 173, 188; William L. Sachs, *The Transformation of Anglicanism*, 324; Welsby, *History of the Church of England*, 111; Carpenter, *Archbishop Fisher*, 304–5.

69. Welsby, *History of the Church of England*, 30.

ment strategy worked well, then parish incumbents would be the direct beneficiaries.[70]

Throughout his archiepiscopate, Geoffrey Fisher maintained a lively and direct involvement in the affairs of the Church Commissioners. Indeed, as the historian Andrew Chandler has written, "of all the archbishops of Canterbury [in the second half of the twentieth century], Fisher alone understood the fundamental significance of the Church Commissioners to the Church of England." Participating in the work of the Commissioners more actively and more knowledgeably than any other archbishop in this fifty-year period, Fisher gave the leaders of the Church Commissioners "the assurance that they acted with authority and that their work did actually stand at the heart of the Church of England."[71] The work of the Commissioners is easily underestimated. As Chandler points out, they became "the great co-ordinating power in the Church, centralizing, reordering, integrating, standardising: stipends, pensions, bishoprics, properties." The modernization of the Church of England was largely their achievement.[72]

The Commissioners retooled the church's investment strategy to maximize earnings (without, at the same time, neglecting ethical considerations). The time had arrived, in the second half of the twentieth century, to move beyond a wasteful, overly cautious approach based on government bonds and on income from low-yielding agricultural lands. Working to establish a more-diversified portfolio, the Church Commissioners bought industrial and commercial shares that promised much higher returns. Income from landowning had been depressed by the holding of long leases at rents that were typically below the market rate. The Church Commissioners addressed this problem either by raising these rents when the leases were renewed, by unloading farmland and investing the revenue in more-profitable ventures, or by selling valuable lands in or near urban

70. Paul, *A Church by Daylight*, 113.

71. Chandler, *The Church of England in the Twentieth Century,* 477–78. Moreover, Fisher worked well with the other key figures who oversaw the Church Commissioners (Sir Malcolm Trustram Eve, Sir James Brown, and Sir Mortimer Warren). Each of these four men, Chandler observes, "appeared to possess what the others lacked. Fisher knew the politics of the Church thoroughly and pragmatically; he saw how new ideas might seem to the people who mattered and, sometimes, how to persuade those whose approval might be necessary in bringing new ventures to life" (46).

72. Ibid., 478. Chandler places the work of the Church Commissioners in its historical setting: This body "came to life in the context of the great Labour governments of 1945–51 and the new primacy" of Geoffrey Fisher; it "was . . . a pragmatic liberal bureaucracy which existed not merely to maintain arrangements but actively to reform them" (4).

areas for commercial or residential development. By no means, however, did the church sever its traditional ties to rural England, as it continued to own more than 1,000 farms.[73]

This new strategy succeeded. From a total income of £7.5 million in the first year of their existence as a combined entity, the Church Commissioners by 1961—Geoffrey Fisher's last year in office—were raising twice that amount per annum.[74] Trevor Beeson likens the amalgamation to a prospering union of husband and wife: "Although the parties to the marriage were somewhat elderly and prim, and although their marriage had been 'arranged' by the Church Assembly, their new life together was vigorous and highly productive."[75] As a result of this success, clergy stipends increased, although salaries continued to be low.[76] Income generated also supported clergy pensions, pensions for their widows, the furnishing and maintenance of parsonages, stipends for cathedral clergy, and the improvement of cathedral buildings.[77] "This reorganization," writes David Edwards, "together with a clear appeal to the laity for new giving, came just in time to rescue the parish clergy from real financial hardship. Fisher, the son of a rector, had never grown out of touch with such facts of life."[78]

Before this practical reform in church finance, wide disparities in clergy pay existed. These differences were not based on the clergyman's needs or his worth; they simply grew out of the differing incomes of the various parish endowments. To reduce extreme inequalities, the Church Commissioners pooled all these endowments and moved to bring about a stipend scale based on fairness. By 1958 the result was a minimum stipend of £550 per year for almost every benefice. The reforms also enabled funds to be directed to maintain clergy and to construct church buildings in the new post-war housing areas.[79]

Although this venture in ecclesiastical reorganization produced unquestionable benefits, it did have a downside. Fisher and the Church

73. Beeson, *The Church of England in Crisis*, 153; Chandler, *The Church of England in the Twentieth Century*, chaps. 2, 4.

74. Beeson, *The Church of England in Crisis*, 153.

75. Ibid.

76. Welsby, *History of the Church of England*, 30.

77. Beeson, *The Church of England in Crisis*, 155; Chandler, *The Church of England in the Twentieth Century*, 2.

78. Edwards, *Leaders*, 361.

79. Beeson, *The Bishops*, 128; Chandler, *The Church of England in the Twentieth Century*, 64–76.

Commissioners had gone a long way in wrenching the church's administration out of the world of Jane Austen and into the modern world of industrial capitalism. But this transformation brought with it a new set of relationships (which the political economist Max Weber would have recognized): increased bureaucratization, a more-centralized administration, more boards and committees. Inevitably, this new machinery could seem impersonal and high-handed, albeit efficient. It "often seem[ed] to the parishes," notes the historian Roger Lloyd, "as though the Church ha[d] become rather like an ecclesiastical civil service, governed not by its bishops but by a string of committees against whose decisions no appeal lies." On the other hand, the steady increase of stipends for the clergy would not have been possible if the Church Commissioners had not had the freedom to take the action that they did. "The price to be paid for skipping a century and a half and bringing the Church's administration suddenly into line with modern requirements was heavy," Lloyd concludes, "but the cost of failure to do it would have been heavier still."[80]

---

80. Lloyd, *The Church of England*, 472.

4

Archbishop of Canterbury, 1945–1961

The Anglican Communion

A Communion of Anglican Churches

A LTHOUGH Geoffrey Fisher indicated that he regarded canon-law reform as his signal contribution to the church, ordinary British men
and women probably identified him most closely with the coronation of
Queen Elizabeth II. Other observers have viewed his historic meeting
with Pope John XXIII as possessing unparalleled significance. But church
historians may be justified in seeing Fisher's work on behalf of the con-
stituent elements of the Anglican Communion as this archbishop's greatest achievement. Promoting the unity-in-diversity of this communion of
autonomous churches was not only something that Fisher did well; it was
an activity that yielded nothing but positive results, both in the present
and for decades to come.

Air travel enabled Fisher to visit the churches of the Anglican
Communion to an extent previously impossible. He traveled all over the
world: to Australia and New Zealand in 1950 (Fisher was the first archbishop of Canterbury to visit the Antipodes), to West Africa in 1951, to
Central Africa in 1955, to India, Pakistan, Japan, Hong Kong, and Korea
in 1959, to Nigeria and East Africa in 1960. His trip with Rosamond
Fisher to Asia in 1959—a strenuous 20,000 miles in five weeks—was the
first tour of Asian countries by an archbishop of Canterbury. Several of
these trips were to inaugurate new provinces of the Anglican Communion.
The new provinces that came into existence after the Second World War—
as well as the jurisdiction of the archbishopric in Jerusalem and the East

Asian Episcopal Conference—got under way during his archiepiscopate and at his urging.[1]

While Fisher has often been described as autocratic, this character-ization may apply more to his manner than to his meaning. He might dominate a discussion, but the aim of the process might well be to turn over authority for the church in portions of Africa or Asia.[2] When evaluat-ing Fisher, we will have to look not only at his methods but also at his purposes and at the results of his work. In the important instance of his efforts on behalf of the Anglican Communion, he was not an autocrat.

Geoffrey Fisher was the archbishop of Canterbury in the waning days of the mighty British Empire, whose heyday was the period from the 1830s to the 1950s. In Africa, before independent states replaced colonies, Fisher had organized four new provinces of the Anglican Communion. This order of events was appropriate, for in many of these countries Anglican missionary activity preceded British rule; the missionary societ-ies were intent upon developing indigenous churches.[3] Not only was the archbishop of Canterbury "ahead of the politicians," notes Trevor Beeson; he aided the statesmen, for this work of establishing autonomous churches "contributed much to the peaceful transition of [these] countries to in-dependence within the Commonwealth."[4] Because Anglican churches achieved autonomy before the countries themselves became politically independent, the newly structured Anglican churches, by virtue of their cohesiveness, provided a practical benefit to the new nations. Moreover, these new provinces signaled an important change in the nature of the Anglican Communion. African and Asian churches increasingly balanced a communion that had been dominated by the Western churches.[5]

Fisher acknowledged that "Anglican" had become a misleading name for the communion, for most of its churches were not English. At a joint session of the American Episcopal Church's General Convention, meet-ing in Philadelphia on September 12, 1946, he declared: "[T]he Anglican Communion embraces many national churches. . . . They are spread all over the world. The name Anglican is already a misnomer; it indicates their remote origin, but it does not at all describe their present condition. They are indigenous churches, not only here and in England and in the

1. *DNB 1971–1980*, s.v. "Fisher, Geoffrey Francis, Baron Fisher of Lambeth."
2. Carpenter, *Cantuar,* 497.
3. Jacob, *The Making of the Anglican Church Worldwide,* 6, 7, 298.
4. Beeson, *The Bishops,* 129.
5. Welsby, *A History of the Church of England, 1945–1980,* 91.

British Dominions, but in India, China, Japan, Ceylon, and Africa, East and West."[6]

The visit to the United States which was the occasion for these remarks was one of many trips that Fisher made as Cantuar. Typically he undertook his travels in order to accomplish definite ends. He visited the United States, for example, not only to greet his American cousins but also—like a savvy politician—to woo them back to Lambeth: the next international conference was but two years away.

Strengthening American Ties

Archbishop Cosmo Lang had made the American bishops feel like outsiders at the Lambeth Conference of 1930.[7] Bishop Henry Knox Sherrill recalled that in 1930 the American bishops felt more like "onlookers" than "participants." Consequently, some of them "said they would not attend another Conference."[8] Aware that this treatment had frayed the ties of friendship, Geoffrey and Rosamond Fisher visited both Canada and the United States in 1946.[9] At the Americans' General Convention, held that year in Philadelphia, Sherrill was elected presiding bishop (taking office on January 1, 1947).

This visit was the first of several trips that Archbishop and Mrs. Fisher would make to North America.[10] Fisher also traveled to the United States for the General Convention of the Episcopal church in 1952.[11] During this visit, on September 7, he gave an address in Christ Church (Old North Church), Boston, which was broadcast over radio and television.[12] In his remarks he said that at the heart of the spiritual heritage of both the United States and Europe "are such things as these: belief that each man

6. GF, "Anglicanism Today," in *The Archbishop Speaks*, 87.

7. Carpenter, *Cantuar*, 497.

8. Quoted in Purcell, *Fisher of Lambeth*, 176. In his autobiography, Sherrill writes: "It was no secret that the American bishops who attended the 1930 Conference came home with the feeling that they had been given scant opportunity to be heard." *Among Friends*, 235.

9. At the end of this visit, Fisher joked with reporters who had covered his trip: "In my 32 days in Canada and the United States," he said, "I have traveled 7,500 miles, I have slept in 22 beds, and I have given 44 sermons. Therefore, for every two sermons I acquired one bed." Ball, "Archbishop Departs from Halifax."

10. Smyth, "In Duty's Path," 69.

11. This visit included a three-week vacation in the Hudson River Valley and Massachusetts with Henry Knox Sherrill and his family. Sherrill, *Among Friends*, 244–45. See "Friends and Bishops," 7.

12. Carpenter, *Cantuar*, 498.

has a personal worth. . . ; belief that man is responsible for his brother's good. . . ; belief that society must be directed first by order and then by freedom, first by duties and then by rights, first by just laws and then by the liberties they secure; belief that society and each member of it is responsible . . . to God."[13] These phrases contain the quintessential Fisherian themes: no real freedom outside an ordered structure, no rights apart from duties, and in all things responsibility to God.

In 1954 Fisher attended the General Assembly of the World Council of Churches in Evanston, Illinois, and the Anglican Congress, held in Minneapolis and chaired by Bishop Sherrill. He was also present for the meeting of the central committee of the World Council of Churches in 1957. In all, he made four visits to the United States.[14]

Fisher had known Sherrill before the latter was the American presiding bishop. "During the war," the archbishop later recalled, "I had formed a great personal friendship with Henry Sherrill. . . . He had been in England in charge of the chaplains looking after the U.S. Forces." The two met for the first time in St. Paul's Cathedral in April 1945. "From then onwards we were completely devoted to each other. . . ." Both leaders worked hard to ensure enthusiastic American participation in the Lambeth Conference of 1948, the first held in eighteen years. The Lambeth Conference was no longer what it had been at the start. Initiated by Archbishop Longley in 1867, for many decades the conference was, Fisher said later, "a little domestic affair," with "comparatively few bishops from overseas." For the 1948 meeting, he wanted "to revive the whole idea of the Lambeth Conference as the great family gathering of the Anglican Communion."[15]

Fisher's genial manner and earnest expression of good will won over the American Episcopalians. Of course, between the 1930 and the 1948 Lambeth conferences was their shared experience of the Second World War, which pulled Britons and Americans closer together. Anyone who peruses the correspondence back and forth between American and British church figures in this period—the letters of deans and theologians, not just of senior prelates—notices this growing bond, strengthened by the writers' awareness not only of a common heritage but also of jointly held principles now under siege. After Lambeth 1948, American Episcopalians had a clearer perception of themselves as an important part of the Anglican

---

13. GF, "Christianity and the Modern World," in Carpenter, *The Archbishop Speaks*, 36.

14. Purcell, *Fisher of Lambeth*, 178. See Sherrill, *Among Friends*, 260–61.

15. Quoted in Purcell, *Fisher of Lambeth*, 174. See Sherrill, *Among Friends*, 201, 236, 240.

Communion, which they could see was—although rather vaguely defined—at least more than a federation of independent churches.

The 1948 Lambeth Conference

The 1948 conference was attended by 326 bishops and ably chaired by Geoffrey Fisher. Among its results were the establishment of the Anglican Congress and the creation of the Anglican Cycle of Prayer, which united Anglicans around the world in prayer each day.[16] Although the agenda of the conference included such weighty topics as the Christian doctrine of man, Christian marriage, church unity, the church in the modern world, and the Anglican Communion, its most important achievement was in the realm of identity and self-awareness.[17]

Stanley Eley, Fisher's senior chaplain, said of the conference: "It was at this time that the Anglican Communion realized that it was a communion. . . . When you have over a hundred United States bishops meeting half a dozen Japanese bishops only three years after the war . . . ended, the emotional currents are bound to be there." But the spirit of fellowship present in this conference channeled these currents in a positive direction: "[S]inking all that in their common Anglican heritage, the fellowship . . . and the love that grew out of that Conference between the various parts of the Anglican Communion welled up again in the Minneapolis Congress of 1954." The tenor of the 1948 conference was established by its presiding officer, Geoffrey Fisher: "Within a very few days," Eley observed, "there was a spirit of informality and yet discipline which is typical, I think, of Fisher."[18]

Arriving in England for this conference, the presiding bishop of the Japanese church, the Right Reverend M. H. Yasiro, brought with him a beautifully embroidered cope as a gift for Cantuar from the women of the Church of Japan. Indeed, it was offered as a peace gesture. But the cope was held up at the docks, its journey blocked by a £200 import fee. After persuading the Chancellor of the Exchequer to cancel this fee, Fisher wore the cope at the opening service of the Lambeth Conference; he wore it again for the coronation of Queen Elizabeth.[19] For this opening

16. Welsby, *History of the Church of England*, 89.
17. Purcell, *Fisher of Lambeth*, 180.
18. Quoted in Purcell, *Fisher of Lambeth*, 181.
19. Purcell, *Fisher of Lambeth*, 181.

service, held on American Independence Day, July 4, 1948, Fisher called on Bishop Sherrill to preach.[20]

Six years later, the spirit of fellowship within the Anglican Communion was further enhanced by the Anglican Congress in Minneapolis, the first meeting of its kind since the Pan-Anglican Congress held in London in 1908. Bringing together both clergy and lay leaders to discuss the communion, the congress sought to stimulate among all participants the recognition that they were responsible for one another. The more-senior members should have special regard for the churches in developing countries which were working toward self-sufficiency.[21] To this gathering each diocese could send one priest and one lay delegate, in addition to its bishops; 657 delegates were present in Minneapolis.[22] Fisher recalled the significance of the celebration of the Eucharist each morning of the congress: "Every morning we met at the Communion service according to a different Anglican liturgy, and that taught all of us a good deal, too. And always there was this atmosphere of loving trust holding us all together in the united spirit of the Anglican Communion."[23]

The 1958 Lambeth Conference

Eventually the 1958 conference turned out well; by this time, many of the bishops knew and trusted one another.[24] But preparations for this gathering had started to go awry when Fisher, following precedent, invited Makarios III (1913–77), among other Orthodox leaders, to attend the opening ceremonies of the conference. Makarios—archbishop of Cyprus from 1950 and Cypriot Greek political leader (he would be elected first president of Cyprus in 1960)—was seen by some in the United Kingdom as a supporter of terrorists. He had, in fact, organized a patriotic youth party that participated in terrorist attacks. When rioting broke out in Cyprus, Turkey, and Greece in 1955, the British, who controlled Cyprus, sent in troops; and in 1956 they exiled Makarios to the Seychelles Islands. Many in the United Kingdom blamed Makarios for the deaths of British soldiers during the

20. Ibid.

21. GF looked forward, he said, to "a new understanding by the older Churches of the loneliness, the lack of resources, the need of leadership and learning felt by many of the younger Churches. Their courage and devotion must stir up the whole Communion to come eagerly to their aid." "Concluding Words," in Dawley, *Report of the Anglican Congress, 1954,* 217.

22. Jacob, *The Making of the Anglican Church,* 278.

23. Quoted in Purcell, *Fisher of Lambeth,* 193.

24. Purcell, *Fisher of Lambeth,* 194. See Sherrill, *Among Friends,* 266–70.

conflict. The feeling was that while Makarios might not have condoned attacks on British troops, he had not condemned them either. To Fisher's relief, a month before the start of the Lambeth Conference, Makarios announced that he would be unable to attend. Earlier, Fisher had gone on television and, during an interview, referred to his fellow-archbishop as "a bad man." This remark got Fisher into further trouble—this time with the Greek Orthodox Christians. Makarios was not only a high-ranking Orthodox official but also the "ethnarch" of the Greeks rebelling against British colonial rule.[25] This whole affair was, in addition, but another instance of Fisher's maladroit handling of the Fourth Estate.

Within Fisher's own ecclesiastical household, a problematic area was the relationship between the two archbishops, York and Canterbury. Just before the start of the Lambeth Conference, Michael Ramsey did something that Fisher thought demonstrated poor judgment: he gave the inaugural address at a eucharistic congress of the Anglo-Catholic organization the Church Union. Fisher thought that Ramsey's prominent participation in this congress was the wrong signal to send at decidedly the wrong time. "At breakfast together," Ramsey's biographer, Owen Chadwick, writes, "Fisher exploded and attacked the Church Union and all that it stood for and said that they had done great harm and ought to apologize." For his part, "Ramsey confessed that they had done a lot of harm and ought to apologize but said that the best of them were trying to, and that the Church of England ought to apologize to the high churchmen for the way in which it had sometimes treated them."[26]

This incident reveals important contrasts between one archbishop of Canterbury and his successor, but Fisher could not allow these differences of churchmanship and personality to get in the way of his conference. In the Lambeth proceedings, Ramsey was to be a key player. The conference would take up the following subjects: the Bible, church unity, progress in the Anglican Communion, resolving conflicts between and within nations, and the family. But the most central of these themes was probably the first, on the authority of the Bible; and Ramsey was chairman of the committee on the Bible and the person who drafted its final report.

Ramsey's group ended up embracing both modern biblical criticism and the authority of the Bible for contemporary life.[27] Fisher was pleased with York's contributions to the conference; and he was especially grateful

25. Edwards, *Leaders of the Church of England, 1828–1978*, 364; Carpenter, *Cantuar*, 507.

26. Chadwick, *Michael Ramsey: A Life*, 98.

27. Ibid., 99.

for the assistance that Ramsey provided in coaxing the Anglo-Catholic participants at Lambeth to take a friendlier attitude toward the Church of South India, which united a church with the historic episcopate to churches without it in a common structure. "Yet," as Owen Chadwick remarks, "nothing could alter the double personal difficulty—a difference of principles between a low churchman and a high churchman, and an indefinable difference of temperament."[28]

It was at this Lambeth conference that Michael Ramsey was widely recognized as an outstanding churchman and as Fisher's likely successor. From the opening service of this gathering, the contrast between the tightly organized and supremely aware Fisher and the frequently abstracted Ramsey would have been apparent to anyone looking out for it: "At the opening service in Canterbury cathedral (3 July 1958)," Chadwick writes, "Ramsey muddled his instructions and wandered all round the cathedral looking for where he was supposed to sit and stand."[29]

Among the other accomplishments of the 1958 Lambeth Conference was a recommendation for the establishment of the Anglican Consultative Council. This body was to carry on the work of the Lambeth Conference between sessions and to advise the archbishop of Canterbury and other bishops. The council began functioning after the 1968 conference. Lambeth also called for a revision of the prayer book. And it blessed the religious communities; the Anglican Communion's official acceptance of monks and nuns made it unique among the churches that came out of the Reformation.[30]

A document that received a good bit of media attention was the report of the Committee on the Family in Contemporary Society, which gave its support to the use of birth control for family planning.[31] Stephen Bayne, the bishop of Olympia, Washington, chaired this committee; his successful handling of this task enhanced his reputation. Fisher voiced his approval of the committee's report. It said:

> [T]he procreation of children is not the only purpose of marriage. Husbands and wives owe to each other and to the depth and stability of their families, the duty to express, in sexual intercourse, the love which they bear and mean to bear to each other. . . . Therefore it is utterly wrong to urge that, unless children are specifically de-

28. Ibid., 100.
29. Ibid., 97.
30. Ibid., 100.
31. Purcell, *Fisher of Lambeth*, 197.

sired, sexual intercourse is of the nature of sin. It is also wrong to say that such intercourse ought not to be engaged in except with the willing intention to procreate children. It must be emphasized once again that Family Planning ought to be the result of thoughtful and prayerful Christian decision. Where it is, Christian husbands and wives need feel no hesitation in offering their decision humbly to God and following it with a clear conscience.[32]

W. M. Jacob notes that this report demonstrated that the bishops "were speaking from a maturely developed moral theology, and with the benefit of personal experience."[33] The church historian E. R. Norman points out that this report represents "quite a volte-face" on the part of the Anglican church, for the 1930 Lambeth Conference had allowed birth control only in cases of exceptional social or medical need. Those qualifications were abandoned. "Contraception," Norman writes, "was now to be freely allowed because of the human values implicit in sexual union. This was a revolution in the church's attitude to sexual morality."[34]

The printed reports of these decennial conferences may or may not be significant or memorable. Stephen Bayne identified what was most important about the Lambeth gatherings when he observed that "Lambeth is like an iceberg; eight-ninths of it invisible (being the conversation and relationships of 320 bishops from all over); and one-ninth (the reports) doesn't give too accurate an idea of the true depth of our meeting."[35] It is significant that the 1958 conference was the first one in which many of those who took part in the "eight-ninths" invisible activity were non-European bishops. The conference was on its way, Adrian Hastings comments, to becoming a truly "international and inter-racial Christian fellowship, rather than an almost accidental imperial and missionary prolongation of the Established Church of the English nation."[36] In sum, especially when viewed in the historical rear-view mirror, what the 1958 Lambeth Conference accomplished was more considerable than is often supposed.[37] When it came time to bring the conference to a close, its president, Geoffrey Fisher, good-naturedly directed some humor at his own

32. Quoted in Purcell, *Fisher of Lambeth*, 198.

33. Jacob, *The Making of the Anglican Church*, 280.

34. Norman, *Church and Society in England, 1770–1970*, 413.

35. Quoted in Booty, *An American Apostle*, 64.

36. Hastings, *A History of English Christianity, 1920–2000*, 449.

37. Jacob, *The Making of the Anglican Church*, 295.

reputation as a headmaster, saying to the members from overseas: "Will those who belong to other forms go back to their classrooms."[38]

Stephen Bayne's appointment as Anglican executive officer was announced by Geoffrey Fisher on April 19, 1959, after Bishop Ambrose Reeves of Johannesburg, South Africa, declined the offer.[39] Fisher and others had become convinced of the need for such an officer, who would travel all over the world, giving further cohesion to the Anglican Communion, helping to hold it together, finding out about and making known the problems and concerns of Anglican churches around the globe.[40] The Lambeth Conference of 1958 created this office. Those who supported the idea recognized that this work needed to be concentrated in the hands of one person, who would have to work well with the archbishop of Canterbury. At the time of Bayne's appointment, the Anglican Communion consisted of 340 dioceses and 40 million church members, including eight million in Africa. There were Anglican prayer books in 170 languages.[41]

New Provinces in Africa

When Geoffrey Fisher became archbishop of Canterbury, there were still many "Overseas Bishops of the Canterbury Jurisdiction," who remained dependent upon Cantuar for oversight. Fisher felt that the time had come for these Anglican churches to reflect in their organization a new maturity and autonomy.[42] He actively assisted them with their formation, personally drawing up the provincial constitutions for the provinces of West Africa, Central Africa, and East Africa. In this process he made use of the model provided by the constitution of the Church in the Province of South Africa. According to its polity, the local archbishop was the focus of unity. He presided over a general synod to which each diocese sent representatives: clergy and laity as well as bishops.[43]

During Fisher's tenure of office, four new provinces were established in Africa: West Africa in 1951, Central Africa in 1955, East Africa in 1960, and Uganda in 1960. Of this achievement, Bishop William Wand commented: "Such a record would alone have been sufficient to make

38. Quoted in Holtby, *Robert Wright Stopford, 1901–1976*, 53.

39. See Peart-Binns, *Ambrose Reeves*, 149, 150, 260.

40. Carpenter, *Archbishop Fisher*, 473.

41. Booty, *An American Apostle*, 92–97; Jacob, *The Making of the Anglican Church*, 279–80.

42. Carpenter, *Archbishop Fisher*, 501.

43. Jacob, *The Making of the Anglican Church*, 268; Carpenter, *Archbishop Fisher*, 500.

Geoffrey Fisher's tenure of the chair of St. Augustine . . . of outstanding importance in the long history of the Anglican Communion."[44]

When Fisher journeyed to West Africa in 1951 it marked the first time that a primate had traveled to inaugurate in person a new province of the Anglican Communion. The Church of the Province of West Africa included the dioceses of Lagos, Sierra Leone, Accra, Niger, the Gambia, and the Rio Pongas. Its formation as a province had been initiated by Archbishop William Temple in 1944. The new province, which brought together—not easily—both Low Church and Anglo-Catholic dioceses, was formally inaugurated by Fisher on April 17, 1951, in Freetown, Sierra Leone, when the bishops of the six dioceses signed the preamble and the articles of the constitution. The archbishop of Canterbury then released them from their oaths of canonical obedience to him, and they elected their own metropolitan.[45] "The granting of independence to the Anglican dioceses in the British West African colonies," notes W. M. Jacob, "took place significantly before they achieved political independence from Britain—Ghana in 1957, Nigeria in 1960 and Sierra Leone in 1961."[46]

In May 1955 Fisher again journeyed to Africa, this time for the inauguration of the new province for Central Africa. Fisher was the celebrant at a Eucharist at the Cathedral of St. Mary and All Saints in Salisbury (the old name of Harare), Southern Rhodesia (now Zimbabwe). This service marked the culmination of a complex process that Fisher had initiated in 1951: the formation of the Church in the Province of Central Africa, consisting of Anglicans in what are now Zimbabwe, Zambia, and Malawi.[47] It was on this trip, during a visit to St. Michael's College in Blantyre, Nyasaland (now Malawi), that Fisher in a discussion with students made his infamous remark that "all men are equal in the love of God but not in the sight of God."[48] His biographer, Edward Carpenter, has commented, "It would be impossible to imagine a form of words more calculated to be misunderstood in so highly charged a political atmosphere. Nor is it easy to understand precisely what this comment means—or was intended to mean."[49] It is just as well that Fisher did not elaborate.

44. Wand, *Anglicanism in History and Today,* 44.

45. Jacob, *The Making of the Anglican Church,* 269.

46. Ibid.

47. Sachs, *The Transformation of Anglicanism,* 315; Jacob, *The Making of the Anglican Church,* 269.

48. Quoted in Carpenter, *Archbishop Fisher,* 518.

49. Carpenter, *Archbishop Fisher,* 518. Hastings comments: "The Archbishop's statement, in so far as it was true, was rather banal, but it was poor theology (Fisher indeed was

In 1960 Fisher, age 73 and still going strong, inaugurated the province of East Africa in a service at Dar es Salaam (a seaport on the Indian Ocean in what is now Tanzania). Consisting of 12 dioceses, this province took longer to form. Also in 1960, Uganda was established as an autonomous province. This transformation, notes W. M. Jacob, had met with "considerable white opposition." Fisher achieved his goal by, in Jacob's words, "forc[ing] the division of the existing diocese into eleven new dioceses, with the suffragans becoming diocesans, and the former diocese becoming a province." Once again, the ecclesiastical realm was ahead of the political, Uganda being formed as an independent province two years before the country gained political independence.[50]

Jacob points out that with the formation of the Uganda province, the Anglican episcopate began to undergo an important change. When 1960 began, there were only three black African diocesans; by the end of that year there were seven. Fisher had consecrated four black African suffragan bishops in 1955; they were made diocesans when Uganda became an autonomous province.[51]

David Edwards points out that Fisher's efforts in Africa amounted to a "double success." His trips "loosened the constitutional" but "strengthened the personal links."[52] Canon Max Warren, general secretary of the Church Missionary Society and an advisor to Fisher on Uganda, later wrote: "In Geoffrey Fisher Africans saw a great church leader, and a European at that, actually abdicating authority, in Africa an event as yet without precedent in the State."[53]

These remarkable developments anticipated the era when the Anglican church in Africa would become one of the largest and strongest forces, and surely one of the most vital elements, in the Anglican Communion. By the end of the twentieth century, the Anglican Communion was no longer largely Anglo-Saxon; by then, most Anglicans did not have English as their first language. Since 1950 the number of provinces had more than doubled, and the fastest-growing dioceses were in Africa and New Guinea.[54] Indeed, by 2006 the average Anglican would not be a middle-aged English gentle-

no theologian) and it could easily be taken as a defence of racial discrimination on the old grounds of God having set each man in his estate—castle or cottage, affluent white suburb or rickety black shanty-town." *History*, 434.

50. Jacob, *The Making of the Anglican Church*, 270.

51. Ibid.

52. Edwards, *Leaders*, 362.

53. Quoted in Edwards, *Leaders*, 362.

54. Jacob, *The Making of the Anglican Church*, 298.

man but a woman of 22 in sub-Saharan Africa walking several kilometers every day to fetch water for her three or four children.[55]

55. Duncan Reid, review of *Beyond Colonial Anglicanism: The Anglican Communion in the Twenty-first Century*, edited by Ian T. Douglas and Kwok Pui-lan, *Journal of Anglican Studies* 3 (2005) 126.

5

Archbishop of Canterbury, 1945–1961

Ecumenical Outreach

As archbishop of Canterbury, Geoffrey Fisher devoted considerable amounts of time and energy to efforts beyond the Anglican
Communion per se: to ecumenical relations with other Christians and
to the various aspects of his role in England as head of the Established
Church.

Fisher was never a brilliant public speaker, and for the most part his
writings are not memorable. Nor was he one of the ecumenical giants
of the twentieth century—devoted to the movement and thoroughly involved in its processes, as William Temple had been or as George Bell was.
Yet Fisher was deeply committed to ecumenism, he played important roles
at key times in its history, and he had good instincts about what should be
done and when. He also had the historical and theological knowledge, the
wide personal acquaintance, and the confidence needed to develop fresh
proposals and to bring them forward in a useful way. And he managed
to carry out this activity while guarding his own flanks. In the customary Anglican fashion, Anglo-Catholics fretted when Fisher reached out to
Protestants, and evangelicals worried when Fisher embraced the Pope.[1]

Moreover, while not known as a wordsmith, Fisher had a politician's
sense of the right phrase at the propitious moment. Perhaps the two phrases that he should be most remembered for relative to ecumenism are "full
communion" and "not return." The first phrase is from the beginning of
his archiepiscopate and relates to Protestants. The latter phrase is from the
end of his tenure of office and relates to the Church of Rome.

1. See Purcell, *Fisher of Lambeth*, 274.

The Cambridge Sermon of 1946

Probably the most famous address of Geoffrey Fisher's entire archiepiscopate is his Cambridge Sermon of 1946. Preached in the University Church
in Cambridge, this sermon stemmed from two factors—two historical
events—one positive and the other negative. The first was the good experience of establishing full communion with the Old Catholics (via the
Bonn Agreement of 1931–32). The second was the bad experience of the
American Episcopalians in trying to bring about an organizational union
with the northern Presbyterians (via a proposal that Fisher deemed too
restrictive).[2]

From these experiences Fisher gained a sense of what in the realm of
church unity was workable and desirable. At a time when ecumenists were
often still thinking merger, Fisher was ahead of his time in wanting to have
unity without submerging ecclesiastical identities. Hence, full communion: a strategy that was to work well in the later decades of the twentieth
century in bringing together Anglicans and Lutherans.

In Britain, little had happened on the ecumenical front after the
Lambeth Conference of 1920 issued its Appeal to All Christian People,
although the churches had come together for social action and in 1942
the British Council of Churches was founded. Unwilling to wait for the
theologians to finish haggling over the theological details of ecumenical agreements, Fisher was ready to start a process aimed at bringing the
Protestant churches of Britain closer together in demonstrable ways.[3] His
proposal did not come completely out of the blue, of course. He had been
in conversation with the Free Churches and had reason to suppose that
they were interested in reopening discussions.

From the pulpit of Great St. Mary's on November 23, in a sermon
entitled "A Step Forward in Church Relations," Fisher proposed that the
churches work toward establishing full communion. This arrangement
would allow churches to exchange clergy, for the orders of all ordained
ministers would be accepted by all participating churches.

"There is a suggestion which I should like . . . to make to my brethren
of other denominations," Fisher said; and then he proposed an institutional relationship somewhere between federation and organic union: "We do
not desire a federation: that does not restore the circulation. [And] we are

2. Carpenter, *Archbishop Fisher*, 310; GF, "Archbishop Fisher's Cambridge Sermon,
1946," in Flindall, *The Church of England, 1815–1948*, 441n4; Peter Staples, "Archbishop
Geoffrey Francis Fisher: An Appraisal," 258. See David Hein, "The Episcopal Church and
the Ecumenical Movement, 1937–1997," 4–13.

3. Welsby, *A History of the Church of England, 1945–1980*, 78.

not yet ready for organic . . . union. But there can be a process of . . . grow-ing alike." Full communion was the best way forward: "What we need is that while the folds remain distinct, there should be a movement towards a free and unfettered exchange of life in worship and sacrament . . . as there is already of prayer and thought and Christian fellowship—in short that they should grow towards that full communion with one another, which already in their separation they have with Christ."[4]

Full communion would be possible only if each church was willing to accept episcopacy. Thus Fisher proposed that the Free Churches consider "taking episcopacy into their own systems."[5] This suggestion was not as bold or presumptuous as it might at first appear, for, as Fisher pointed out, the Free Churches had already said that any future united church would be episcopal, in some form. Cantuar noted that the Church of England was already in full communion with the Old Catholics on the Continent, "and," he added, "its relations with the Orthodox Churches . . . and with the Churches of Sweden and Finland . . . approach . . . full communion."[6]

Fisher's manner helped to make his message more palatable. A Free Churchman who was present recalled, "He was so simple and unaffected in his style, so brotherly and cordial in his attitude that he won all hearts."[7] The Free Churches responded favorably to Fisher's sermon, agreeing to hold conversations with representatives of the Church of England. These discussions took place over the next five years.[8]

Roger Lloyd sums up the significance of Fisher's Cambridge Sermon: "How much is owed to [this sermon] is hardly possible even to guess, but it did take the movement out of the deep freeze and got inter-church discussions started again. There is surely a connection between the sermon and the new proposals for communion and finally organic unity between the Methodist Church and the Church of England."[9] In the final chapter of this biography we will see what Fisher's reaction was to these proposals

---

4. GF, "Archbishop Fisher's Cambridge Sermon," in Flindall, *The Church of England, 1815–1948*, 438.

5. See the comments on this proposal by Vincent Taylor, principal of Wesley College, Headingley, Leeds, in "Living Issues in Biblical Scholarship," 271–74.

6. GF, "Archbishop Fisher's Cambridge Sermon," in Flindall, *The Church of England, 1815–1948*, 438.

7. Quoted in Carpenter, *Archbishop Fisher*, 311.

8. Welsby, *History of the Church of England*, 79; Carpenter, *Cantuar: The Archbishops in Their Office*, 503.

9. Lloyd, *The Church of England, 1900–1965*, 470.

for eventual union when they came forward during the archiepiscopate of his successor and former pupil, Michael Ramsey.

The World Council of Churches

Fisher had been active in the British Council of Churches since its inception during the war. The British Council brought together members of 16 denominations: the Church of England, the Church in Wales, the Church of Ireland, the Free Churches, the Salvation Army, the Society of Friends, and five interdenominational organizations. As bishop of London Fisher had served as chairman of the BCC's executive committee; from 1945 to 1961, as Cantuar, he served as the council's president.

The Church of England had been among the earliest supporters of international ecumenism, starting with the World Missionary Conference held in Edinburgh in 1910.[10] Geoffrey Fisher played a significant role in the World Council of Churches—the first international, interdenominational Christian consultative body—from its earliest days.[11] In fact, it was Fisher who was in the chair of the Assembly when the WCC was formally inaugurated on August 23, 1948, in Amsterdam. On this historic occasion, 351 delegates from 147 churches were in attendance. Among the major religious bodies, only the Roman Catholic Church and the Orthodox churches within the Soviet orbit did not send representatives.[12]

At this meeting, Fisher was immediately elected one of the World Council's presiding officers.[13] The WCC had decided to have a five-man collegial presidency, making the office of president more symbolic than substantive. The president functioned more or less as a parliamentary chairman, while the real administrative authority was held by the general secretary (Willem A. Visser 't Hooft) and by the committee chairmen.[14]

On September 1, 1952, *Time* magazine published an article that usefully incorporated Geoffrey Fisher's views on the role of the World Council of Churches. The author of this article noted that Fisher "favors church unity—as an ideal. But, practically speaking, he has his reservations." Cantuar is quoted as saying that the WCC "is not a church. It is none of its business to negotiate a reunion between the churches." And if the World Council of Churches tried to force any changes in the creed of

10. Welsby, *History of the Church of England*, 92.

11. Purcell, *Fisher of Lambeth*, 189.

12. Welsby, *History of the Church of England*, 92.

13. Staples, "Archbishop Geoffrey Francis Fisher," 257.

14. Warren, *Theologians of a New World Order*, 119.

the Anglican church, then "we should clear out." The author of this piece concluded, "In this ultimate stubbornness, the archbishop is supported by most Anglican churchmen. In his quiet way, . . . Fisher has intensified the predilection of his flock for their middle way in Christendom, and has added to their confidence that it is a true way, a good compromise between Geneva and Rome."[15]

Billy Graham's Greater London Crusade, 1954

Cantuar was a supporter of Billy Graham's famous London Crusade of 1954. Fisher said of it: "The mission has beyond doubt brought new strength and hope in Christ to multitudes, and won many to Him; and for this God is to be praised."[16] He believed that the churches could learn something from Graham's methods. "So often," he asserted, the churches "do not begin far enough back. They expect people to understand whole sentences of church life and doctrine before they have been taught the letters of the Christian alphabet and the words of one syllable." That's a natural mistake. But "Dr. Graham has taught us all to begin again at the beginning of our evangelism and speak by the power of the Holy Spirit of sin and of righteousness and of judgment."[17]

Initially cool toward Graham's mass meeting, Fisher warmed to it by the time the crusade ended. He appeared with Graham on the platform of the final meeting at the Empire Stadium, in Wembley. Moved by what he had seen and heard, Fisher turned to the evangelist Grady Wilson and said, "We'll never see such a sight again until we get to heaven!" Enthusiastically putting his arm around Fisher's shoulder, Wilson told him, "That's right, Brother Archbishop, that's right!"[18]

Journey to Jerusalem

The idea for his last major trip as archbishop came to Geoffrey Fisher "in one flash . . . in my study."[19] He determined to go first to Jerusalem, then to Istanbul, and finally to Rome. Meeting with the heads of the Orthodox churches on their home turf was the natural next step in a developing relationship that included Fisher's friendship with Archbishop Germanos,

15. *Time*, September 1, 1952, 53.

16. GF, "A Remarkable Campaign," in Cook, *London Hears Billy Graham*, viii.

17. Ibid., viii–ix.

18. Dudley-Smith, *John Stott*, 299.

19. Purcell, *Fisher of Lambeth*, 270.

the official representative of the Ecumenical Patriarch in London. In July 1956 nine Anglican and 12 Russian theologians and church leaders had met in Moscow for a theological conference.[20] Thus much important groundwork had already been laid, at least for the Orthodox stages of this journey.

In Jerusalem, in November 1960, Fisher met with the Patriarch of Jerusalem, Benedictus, with both the Latin and the Armenian patriarchs, with the governor of Jerusalem, and with the Franciscan Custodian of the Holy Places. He preached in the Anglican Cathedral of St. George and visited the traditional pilgrimage places.[21]

The scholar of ecumenism will note the advances that this trip brought about in Anglican-Orthodox relations. But the student of Fisher's life may find one incident of greatest interest. It occurred at one of these traditional pilgrimage sites. Fisher was a typical English ecclesiastic in his reluctance to wear his religion on his sleeve. He would expect an observer to infer his faith from his obvious commitment to Christianity in its traditional, orthodox, institutional expressions—that is, from his participation in its rituals, from his involvement with its sacred texts, from his preaching and sacramental actions, even from his strenuous efforts in church administration. The rest would be private. To the student of his life, signs of something else going on may be welcome, therefore, when they do occur.

On a visit to the Church of the Holy Sepulchre, Fisher had what may be best characterized as a deeply felt experience of participation in the Body of Christ—in the eucharistic sense in which Body of Christ means both Jesus Christ, crucified and risen, and the body of Christian believers. Fisher's experience was so intense that his normally accurate and detailed memory could not capture the entirety of this occurrence. "I cannot describe the church," he said later. "I hardly saw it. I remember the first place I knelt—a stone on which Our Lord's body was supposed to have rested after being taken down from the cross. Why can I not recall all of this with exactitude? Because throughout, in a strange way, I became mentally passive, feeling a kind of victim with Our Lord." From the moment that Geoffrey Fisher entered the church, he was surrounded by Orthodox monks, Franciscan friars, and others, who virtually carried him from place to place, holding up his arms. There were many steps down to the chapels and then up to the sepulcher. Fisher said that he scarcely walked. Carried along by Orthodox, Franciscans, and Armenians, he hardly had a chance

---

20. Staples, "Archbishop Geoffrey Francis Fisher," 259.

21. See Herklots, *Frontiers of the Church*, 80.

to stumble. "At a place I would kneel and feel Our Lord looking at us in this strange mixture of past and present; then be borne on again, this way and that, and feeling lovingly at their mercy. And I felt that somehow like this Our Lord was pulled and hustled and felt at the mercy of his unloving guides." Beyond this powerful sense of being both with Christ and with Christ's followers, Fisher could not recall much at all. "At intervals the bells would clang again. The whole thing was an astonishing outpouring of every kind of excited motion, all flowing round and over me, not me as a person, but as a kind of center point of that triumphal showing forth of Christian fellowship."[22]

From Jerusalem, Fisher journeyed to Istanbul, where he met with Athenagoras I, the Ecumenical Patriarch, head of the Orthodox churches throughout the world.[23] These face-to-face encounters between Fisher and Orthodox leaders helped to move forward Anglican-Orthodox relations. Fisher's visits were an important prelude to the decision taken at the Pan-Orthodox Conference at Rhodes in 1964 to pursue doctrinal discussions with Anglicans. Moreover, Fisher's efforts dovetailed with the interests and commitments of the archbishop of York, Michael Ramsey, who loved the Orthodox tradition and relished participating in theological dialogues with Orthodox churchmen.

Meeting the Pope

Geoffrey Fisher's historic visit with Pope John XXIII occurred on December 2, 1960. It took place in a changed ecumenical context. Pope John had called for a Council of the Universal Church, which would become known as Vatican II (1962–65); and the pope had established, as a part of the preparation for this council, a new Secretariat for the Promoting of Unity among Christians. In August 1959, the secretary of this new body, Monsignor Jan Willebrands, as an unofficial Roman Catholic observer, attended a meeting of the Central Committee of the World Council of Churches, held at St. Andrews, Scotland.[24] Fisher talked with Willebrands on this occasion, and shortly thereafter the pope communicated his willingness to meet Cantuar at the Vatican.[25] Fisher's visit was to be one of the

22. Quoted in Purcell, *Fisher of Lambeth*, 277.

23. Fisher was only the second archbishop of Canterbury to visit an Ecumenical Patriarch, after Lang in 1939.

24. Carpenter, *Cantuar*, 501.

25. Staples, "Archbishop Geoffrey Francis Fisher," 260; Carpenter, *Archbishop Fisher*, 707.

first initiatives undertaken in response to this new ecumenical openness on the part of the Church of Rome.[26]

But Vatican officials still viewed Cantuar's visit with suspicion, handling it, in the words of one Vatican scholar, "like a guilty secret."[27] In announcing this historic event, the first such visit since Archbishop Arundel's in 1397, the official Vatican newspaper, *Osservatore Romano*, simply referred to the archbishop of Canterbury as "Dr. Fisher."[28] After failing to prevent this visit, Vatican officials suppressed the media coverage as much as possible.[29] The visit would be known, as *Osservatore Romano* phrased it, as *una semplice visita di cortesia*: a simple visit of courtesy. When Fisher arrived for his audience with the pope, his escort rushed him by the Swiss guards and permitted no photographs to be taken of the archbishop and the pope together. Still, Fisher's audience with the pope was unusually long: 67 minutes.[30]

For his part, Geoffrey Fisher—from the Protestant wing of the Anglican church—also had some history to deal with. He later recalled, "I grew up with an inbred opposition to anything that came from Rome. I objected to their doctrine; I objected to their methods of reasoning; I objected to their methods of operation in this country."[31]

What changed his attitude? "Without any doubt, the personality of Pope John. It was quite obvious to the world that Pope John was a different kind of pope, whom I should like to meet, and could meet, on grounds of Christian brotherhood without any kind of ecclesiastical compromise on either side. Of this I felt certain already."[32]

When Fisher and Pope John met, the archbishop recalled, the pope, in the course of their discussion, "quoted to me a passage from a recent

26. Welsby, *History of the Church of England*, 177.

27. Nichols, *The Politics of the Vatican*, 314.

28. Carpenter, *Archbishop Fisher*, 708.

29. Welsby, *History of the Church of England*, 177.

30. Chadwick, *Michael Ramsey*, 319.

31. Quoted in Purcell, *Fisher of Lambeth*, 271. An example of one such doctrinal difference was the Roman Catholic dogma of the Bodily Assumption of the Blessed Virgin Mary. In his address to the full synod of the Convocation of Canterbury in 1950, GF made his views clear: "We [Cantuar and the archbishop of York] cannot understand their [Roman Catholics'] insistence on requiring acceptance within their own ranks of doctrines altogether outside the Bible and the ancient universal creeds." Promulgating such dogma, Fisher believed, "leads only to the confusion of Christian truth when Roman Catholic theologians draw inference from inference, far removed from any evidence, historical or otherwise." President's Address, September 12, 1950, *Chronicle of Convocation, 1950*, 355.

32. Quoted in Purcell, *Fisher of Lambeth*, 273.

address of his in which as it happened occurred a reference to the time when his 'separated brethren' would return to the Church of Rome." When he heard this language being used, Fisher interrupted the pope with a momentous, if brief, word of—one might say—correction: "I said, 'Your Holiness, not *return*.'" Taken aback, the pope asked his interlocutor to explain what he meant. Fisher replied, "None of us can go backwards, only forwards. Our two Churches are advancing on parallel courses and we may look forward to their meeting one day." After a pause, the pope said, "'You are quite right' and I never heard him speak again of our 'returning.'"[33]

"Not *return*": With that brief interjection Fisher made it clear that he, on behalf of the Anglican Communion, must reject a musty approach to ecumenism which spoke only of separated and errant brethren "returning" to the One True Church. This meeting was played down by the Vatican officials, but unquestionably it marked the beginning of a new relationship between the two ancient churches—and on new terms. A man who undertook this journey "late in my life, late in my experience of Christian faith and living," Geoffrey Fisher deserves much credit for keeping his wits about him and for making of this meeting much more than a bland exchange of courtesies.[34]

Following this trip and in anticipation of the Second Vatican Council, Cantuar in 1961 dispatched to Rome a representative, Canon Bernard Pawley of Ely Cathedral, to note the preparations for the council and to be available to the Secretariat for Unity to provide information about the Church of England. The two churches, Fisher believed, needed to understand each other as well as possible. These years, when Cardinal John Heenan was archbishop of Westminster and Eugene Cardinale was the apostolic delegate, saw an improvement in Anglican-Roman Catholic relations in Britain.[35]

The Second Vatican Council appears to have recognized this new relationship. In its decree on ecumenism it gives special recognition to the Anglican Communion: "Among [the churches separated from the holy see] in which some catholic traditions and institutions continue to exist, the Anglican communion occupies a special place."[36] Roger Lloyd offers this comment on the meeting of Fisher and the pope in relation to Vatican II: "No one can say, and it would be impertinent to guess, just what was

33. GF, *Touching on Christian Truth*, 187–88.

34. GF, quoted in Lloyd, *The Church of England*, 587.

35. Welsby, *History of the Church of England*, 178.

36. Decree on Ecumenism, in Abbott, *The Documents of Vatican II*, 356, §13.

the effect of this famous meeting between these two kind, genial, but very different men. The Second Vatican Council might very well have taken just the same course as in fact it did if they had never met at all." But, he notes, "From the English side [this meeting and its aftermath] kindled a respect, even an affection, for Rome which had not existed for centuries before."[37]

Fisher himself, in retirement, continued to look forward to progress with Rome. He kept up his contacts with leading Roman Catholics, corresponding and conversing with them, always seeking greater Christian unity. He did not seek union with Rome. But with his English Roman Catholic friends he hopefully discussed possible approaches to full communion.[38]

What had Fisher learned from this last trip of his archiepiscopate? Or at least, what was his most vivid memory? Interviewed upon landing in London on December 3, 1960, Fisher said that his strongest memory was of "a camel which looked at me with most ineffable scorn. A donkey smiles. Roughly speaking, all humanity is a donkey or a camel."[39] A simple parable but one that may indicate why the pope and the archbishop got on as well as they did.

Coda: Reaching Out to Non-Christians

Ecumenism, the subject of this chapter, typically refers to efforts to achieve unity among the various Christian bodies. The term does not denote inter-religious dialogue, which appears to have engaged Geoffrey Fisher's attention to no appreciable degree. But there was a large and perhaps growing population of non-Christians in Britain whom Cantuar could not fail to take note of: men and women all around him, alienated or secularized countrymen to whom Christian beliefs were literally incredible. Did the archbishop of Canterbury have anything to say to them? Were all these doubters simply beyond the pale of God's kingdom and therefore damned forever? Not a bit of it. Fisher's attitude toward these non-Christians was decidedly irenic and understanding.

In 1959 an interviewer asked him about those persons who try to follow the ethical teachings of Jesus but who cannot believe in the divinity of Christ or even in the existence of God. What about them? Cantuar replied that if they can accept only Christ's moral teaching, then they should try to live by these principles: "Christ will be with them in their honest

37. Lloyd, *The Church of England*, 587.
38. Arblaster, "'All the world's a stage . . . ,'" 46.
39. Quoted in Purcell, *Fisher of Lambeth*, 268.

endeavour." A Christian, he said, respects those who live good lives, even though these individuals do not accept the divinity of Christ. Although they are not believers, they "are walking in the Light of Christ." For both Christians and non-Christians, Fisher observed, "there is only one true Light of the world. . . . Christ is the Light of the World and He rejoices . . . when non-Christians walk in it." And so, Cantuar suggested, "in the Kingdom of God, there is . . . a place for the agnostic, as there certainly is for the sinner." It was the atheist whom Fisher could not understand. "The atheist says there is not, there cannot be, God or a Kingdom of God: his reason tells him so. But reason doesn't. Reason cannot prove that there is not a God, any more than it can prove finally that there is."[40]

At this point Fisher drew both a distinction and a connection between faith as Christian belief and faith as the walk or life of a Christian: The believer has weighed the probabilities and made an "inner choice," but that is not the end of the affair. In living the life of faith the Christian grows into a deeper understanding of God's purposes and indeed into a deeper awareness of God's own life. God may in a sense still be a hypothesis, "since we walk by faith and not by sight," but Christian conviction increasingly becomes a "certainty beyond a peradventure." The test of Christian truth-claims cannot be made at the very beginning, apart from life, in an antiseptic laboratory, but only in the muck of one's actual existence, with all its challenges, griefs, joys, travails, loves, and repentances.[41]

This connection between faith and life has ramifications for those who have trouble with Christian belief. At least, Fisher said, such persons can "believe in the purpose of Christ and the kind of creative life He exhibited, and the Kingdom which He preached." They can make Christ's loving and healing purpose their own commitment. What happens next? Then "they will be so busy *doing* these creative things, or rather finding out by trial and error what to do and how to do it, that they will not spend too much time asking and answering questions (which becomes sometimes an excuse for not committing oneself)." Fisher pointed out that "Our Lord said, 'Come, follow Me' into this creative pattern of responsible life. If they do that they will almost certainly find that they come to believe" in the overcoming of brokenness and the raising of new life through Christ, and hence come to know the meaning in and for their own lives of the Crucifixion and Resurrection of Christ.[42] "Doctrine and life," Fisher wisely

40. GF, quoted in Harris, *Conversations*, 81–82.

41. Ibid., 82.

42. Ibid., 82–83.

noted, "come to be inextricably part of the same loyalty, each connecting the other and informing it."[43]

43. Ibid., 84.

6

Archbishop of Canterbury, 1945–1961

Church and State

The Established Church

In the Fisher era, the church historian E. R. Norman observes, "The principle of Established religion was very much taken for granted. . . . During the 1940s and 1950s very few within the Church of England questioned it; and the few Nonconformists or secularists who spoke of disestablishment were responding to historical instincts which were not live politics . . . ." Both William Temple and Geoffrey Fisher "assumed the existence of the National Church. . . . Nearly every leading churchman in these years felt the same."[1]

This principle of Church Establishment which was so widely accepted has traditionally been interpreted in such a way that it has more to say about responsibility than about authority; it has more to do with reciprocal obligations than with special privileges. It signifies, on the one hand, the responsibility of the state to God; and, on the other hand, the responsibility of the Church of England to all the people of the land, whether they are Anglicans or not. Cyril Garbett devoted much energy to working out what Establishment properly stands for. "The Church of England," he said in 1947, "still in many ways represents the religious aspect of the nation. This is most notably seen at the Coronation. . . . The Church, hallowing the King, calls upon the State to remember that it is

---

1. Norman, *Church and Society in England, 1770–1970*, 397. As GF put it, "the Free Churches have discovered that the Establishment has positive advantage both for them and for the country as serving well the whole place of the Christian religion in the life of the nation." GF, "Church and State," in *Touching on Christian Truth*, 140.

the servant of the spiritual order, and that all its power and glory are a trust from God to be used for His purposes."[2]

At the same time, as Garbett said in 1950 in his book on the relationship of church and state, the Church of England is specially obliged to look after the spiritual welfare of the nation. "It is one of the glories of the Church that its clergy minister not only to a congregation, but to all who live within the parish."[3] The church has a "duty of making spiritual provision for the whole nation. . . ."[4] Beyond providing pastoral care, representatives of the Church of England have a duty to give moral guidance to the state on a wide range of questions. "An Established Church," Garbett wrote, "has the responsibility of arousing and educating the conscience of the State and the nation on matters of public policy and administration. It must show that Christianity has a message not only to the individual but also to society. It must proclaim God's laws of justice, mercy, and love, and at the same time show their relevance to current politics."[5]

Recognizing that public-policy questions have ethical and theological ramifications, Geoffrey Fisher frequently spoke out, in Parliament and elsewhere, on the issues of his time: artificial insemination, nuclear weapons, the British invasion of Egypt during the Suez Crisis, premium bonds, the death penalty, and other controversial subjects. Although he was politically to the right of his predecessor, William Temple, he accepted the Welfare State. But he warned against the danger of too much state control and the consequent loss of concern for the whole person: the moral and spiritual as well as the physical and material needs of human beings.[6]

Fisher was not an uncritical admirer of Conservative governments. In fact, he got along best with the Labour premier Clement Atlee and

2. Garbett, *The Claims of the Church of England*, 189, 190.

3. Garbett, *Church and State in England*, 129. "[E]very citizen lives in some parish," Fisher wrote, ". . . and can claim the spiritual counsel and ministrations of the parish priest; and this pastoral duty of the clergy . . . still remains as the first care and privilege of the Church." GF, "The Beliefs of the Church of England," in *The Archbishop Speaks*, 55.

4. Garbett, *Church and State in England*, 130.

5. Ibid., 131. When he was enthroned as archbishop of Canterbury on April 19, 1945, GF said, "All through our history . . . the Church has been organically related to the nation, charged with the duty of bringing into the secular life of our people the sanctities of the faith and fear of God, by teaching them to fashion their characters and their policies by the obedience which Christians owe to their Lord. For long indeed Church and nation were different names for the same body of people, the one describing them on the side of their heavenly, and the other of their earthly citizenship." GF, "Church and Nation," in Smyth, *The Church and the Nation*, 13.

6. Purcell, *Fisher of Lambeth*, 210; Norman, *Church and Society*, 377.

least well with a Tory politician, Harold Macmillan (who did better with Fisher's successor, Michael Ramsey). Fisher criticized Macmillan on matters related to both domestic and foreign policy. The archbishop found particularly distasteful the Conservative premier's 1959 campaign slogan, "You Never Had It So Good." He labeled this phrase "dreadful," saying it was used to justify "a smug contentment which ignores the peril of our own situation and the appalling conditions of people in other countries."[7]

While Temple was an idealistic man of the Left, Fisher tended to be a hard-nosed, common-sense realist, whose instincts were fundamentally conservative. Fisher supported the death penalty in certain cases of murder, for example, and attributed this stance to his belief in the dignity of human life and in the right of society to defend itself.[8] Thus Christie Davies, writing in 2004 on the "death of moral Britain," considers this archbishop an emblematic "reminder of a social and moral world we have lost and of the strange death of Conservative England, despite the decisive victory of capitalism over socialism."[9] Fisher was indeed a respecter of authority and of established institutions, as well as firmly anti-Communist. Referring to Cantuar's famous remark to Pope John, David L. Edwards says of Fisher, "Although with his head he knew that 'none of us can go backwards,' he was at heart content with the Establishment he had entered on becoming

7. GF to R. A. Butler, February 16, 1960, R. A. Butler Papers (Trinity College, Cambridge), G35, fols. 39–43, quoted in Jefferys, *Retreat from New Jerusalem*, 198–99. For his part, Macmillan characterized GF as "silly, weak, vain and muddle-headed." Macmillan, *The Macmillan Diaries*, 577 (entry for July 21, 1956). He also found Fisher to be an unengaging conversation partner: "I try to talk to [Cantuar] about religion," the premier commented in his diary. "But he seems to be quite uninterested and reverts all the time to politics." *The Macmillan Diaries*, entry for February 8, 1957, quoted in Hennessy, *Having It So Good*, 502.

       Hennessy points out, however, that Fisher and Macmillan had much in common. Both had misgivings about the moral changes taking place in British society. "Fifties Britain," notes Hennessy, "tends to be viewed through early-twenty-first-century eyes as stuffy and staid, but for Macmillan's and Fisher's generation, their standard of a tranquil, self-ordering society was that of pre-1914 England" (517). A devout Anglican, Macmillan worried about the spiritual costs of "having it so good" (516). To an interviewer in 1959, Fisher spoke with concern about the multiplication in an affluent society of "temptations to self-indulgence (which accounts for a great deal of the world's sin and misery)" and about the weakening of "many of the time-honoured defences against bad thinking and bad doing." GF, quoted in Harris, *Conversations*, 85.

8. GF Papers 167, fols. 201 and 204 (March 8, 1956).

9. Davies, "The British State and the Power of Life and Death," 374. See Davies, *The Strange Death of Moral Britain*, 67–78, 113–14, 117; and Potter, *Hanging in Judgment*, 124, 151, 166, 168–69, 178–79, 193. Capital punishment would be abolished in Britain in 1969.

a headmaster less than ninety years after Thomas Arnold, and he was confident that this old England could be brought alive by hard work—such as
he himself gave without stint all his life."[10]

Sex and Marriage

Fisher's essential conservatism displayed itself whenever a topic came up
that had anything to do with sex. For example, in the late 1940s, he saw
AID (Artificial Insemination by Donor) as immoral, even suggesting
that it be made a criminal offense. He reasoned that AID was a breach
of the marriage contract, a violation of the exclusive relationship between
husband and wife.[11] A decade later, Fisher held the same views. In his
presidential address to the full synod of the Convocation of Canterbury
in January 1958, Fisher said that if AID were not made a crime, then at
least some legal restrictions ought to be imposed upon it, including the
registration of the names of donors.[12]

Fisher upheld—indeed insisted upon—the church's traditional teaching on marriage and divorce. He became archbishop at the beginning of
a period of rapid increase in the divorce rate. From 1.5 per 10,000 in
1938, the number of divorces shot up to 13.6 per 10,000 in 1947. Both
liberalized divorce laws and the turmoil of war help to account for this
steep rise.[13] When a Labour Member of Parliament sought approval for allowing a seven-year period of marital separation to count as an additional
ground for divorce, Fisher condemned the proposal as a sop to a morally
sick society bent on rejecting marriage for life.[14]

The archbishop supported the position of the Convocations in for-
bidding the clergy from holding a second marriage in the church.[15] When

10. Edwards, *Leaders of the Church of England, 1828–1978,* 365–66.

11. Machin, *Churches and Social Issues in Twentieth-Century Britain,* 155; Purcell, *Fisher of Lambeth,* 213–14; Carpenter, *Archbishop Fisher,* 391–92; *Church Times,* July 30, 1948, 423.

12. GF, "President's Address," January 14, 1958, in *Chronicle of Convocation 1958,* 4. See GF Papers 235, fol. 140, and two newspaper cuttings that follow: one from the *Daily Mail,* the other from the *Daily Mirror,* both articles from January 21, 1960; Purcell, *Fisher of Lambeth,* 214; Carpenter, *Cantuar,* 506.

13. Machin, *Churches and Social Issues,* 149.

14. Ibid., 150. Fisher's position was absolute and unbending. He was distressed, for example, by Anthony Eden's remarriage after divorce, even though Cantuar acknowledged the absence of any moral error on Eden's part. GF to Peter Winckworth, October 8, 1952, GF Papers 99, fol. 299; Thorpe, *Eden,* 378.

15. See his statement on the remarriage of the divorced in the *Chronicle of Convocation 1957,*

Princess Margaret wanted to marry Group Captain Peter Townsend—who had been the innocent party in the dissolution of his marriage—Fisher made it clear what the church's position was. On October 27, 1955, Margaret had an hour-long private conference with the archbishop in his study. Four days later she issued a press statement which said that she was "mindful of the Church's teaching that marriage is indissoluble" and that she would not be marrying the Group Captain.[16]

People naturally supposed that Fisher had put some pressure on the princess to call off the marriage, an allegation that the archbishop vehemently denied. But "it is scarcely likely," observes a biographer of Queen Elizabeth II, "that the purpose of such a meeting *à deux* between a Primate and a Princess at such a time was to make small-talk, and the Archbishop was not reticent about his firmly held opinions on the subject of divorce and re-marriage."[17]

In the event, Margaret married Antony Armstrong-Jones, and of course that marriage failed. Would she have been better off with the Group Captain? In hindsight, it is easy to wish that Fisher had been more attentive to the human beings involved and less beholden to his sense of what the rules were in this case. The breakdown of Princess Margaret's marriage, writes Ben Pimlott, "carried the savage message that the Archbishop, the editor of the *Times*, the Cabinet and other moralizers who had advised the Queen about Peter Townsend's suit had, in human terms, been wrong; and that the Queen might have done better to have stood up to them."[18] It is impossible now to disagree with that conclusion.

Premium Bonds

In the mid 1950s an issue of personal morality and state policy arose which sharply divided Geoffrey Fisher and the Conservative Government. "It was when [Fisher] touched on the question of Premium Bonds," writes William Purcell, "that he became formidable, launching out into a tremendous polemic, which was neither forgotten nor forgiven by some in the Government of the day."[19]

208.

16. Norman, *Church and Society*, 411.

17. Pimlott, *The Queen*, 236.

18. Ibid., 437.

19. Purcell, *Fisher of Lambeth*, 215. See Harold Macmillan's comments in *The Macmillan Diaries*, 554 (entry for April 26, 1956).

Announced on April 17, 1956, as part of Chancellor of the Exchequer Harold Macmillan's budget proposals, premium bonds were designed as a way to reduce inflation and to encourage savings by those who might be attracted by the prospect of winning cash prizes. Interest earned by investors' money would go not to the individual bondholders but toward a pool of cash awards. Bondholders, in other words, were gambling with their interest payments, which were collected into a central fund and then awarded as prizes. The first premium bond was purchased on November 1, 1956. By the end of that day, men and women, in pursuit of the top prize of £1,000, had spent £5 million on premium bonds. The first drawing was held on June 1, 1957; by then £82 million had been invested. People participated in Macmillan's new state savings scheme not only because there was no risk—their initial capital investment was inviolate; it could be recovered at any time—but also because it was one of the few games in town.

Because the cash prizes were distributed by chance, the scheme met with opposition from those, including the British Council of Churches, who viewed it as gambling. The government, Geoffrey Fisher said in the House of Lords, "have chosen . . . a rather second-rate expedient, which may attract savings but which adds nothing to the spiritual capital of the nation," relying as it does on "motives of private gain." Fisher was against "[p]rivate gain divorced from responsibility," and so he was against premium bonds. The government should be certain "that money gained shall be truly earned and that money earned shall be used reasonably, thoughtfully and for the general good."[20] Fisher's challenge to the government drew few others in Parliament to his side, however, and of course the government's proposal was adopted.[21]

Nuclear Weapons

In his attitude to the use of nuclear bombs Geoffrey Fisher displayed his essential realism. He deplored the awful nature of these weapons but acknowledged that the West was facing an enemy both remorseless and relentless, who would stop at nothing, except equal or greater counterforce. Responding to a Sheffield union leader who urged the church to "raise her voice [against] these horrible weapons," Fisher affirmed his belief that

20. GF, Speech on the Small Lotteries and Gaming Bill, April 26, 1956, *The Parliamentary Debates (Hansard): House of Lords Official Report* (London: Her Majesty's Stationery Office, 1957) 196:1303–4.

21. Machin, *Churches and Social Issues*, 148–49.

"[t]he greatest difficulty is that the Soviet government openly proclaims that it does not believe in God or in spiritual laws, or in prayer or in the obligation of men and nations to seek peace and ensure it. Thus, there is a fundamental distrust created in the nature of things." Nuclear weapons are needed, therefore, as a deterrent and a bargaining lever: "It may be that the existence of the H-Bomb will be a more powerful agent in leading to some kind of agreement than anything else."[22] Because he held Soviet Communism to be a real threat to freedom and world peace, he would not go along with those who called for a ban on nuclear weapons. He saw nuclear weapons as a tragic but necessary resource in the world as it actually existed.[23]

Fisher was a Cold War—and Church of England—realist. When George Bell wrote to *The Times* on April 5, 1954, arguing against nuclear weapons, Cantuar told the bishop of Winchester, "I have a horrible feeling that there ought to be a motion down on the Convocation Agenda about the Hydrogen Bomb. It is not that anything we say will do anybody any conceivable good, but if we say nothing there will be protests that the Church gives no lead and that when the world is in jeopardy talks about nothing but its own Canons."[24]

The Convocation did express its apprehension about the hydrogen bomb, calling the existence of this new weapon "a grievous enlargement of the evil inherent in all war and . . . a threat to . . . humanity and civilisation." But the Convocation also recognized that "statesmen[,] in the discharge of their responsibilities and in the existing conflict of international interests and beliefs, cannot separate consideration of the Hydrogen Bomb from that of other weapons of war or from the total state of international relations"—thus appearing to accept the maintenance of these weapons for as long as the conflict lasted. The motion called upon "all statesmen urgently to seek agreement" on the reduction and control of arms.[25]

The church's official pronouncements continued to come in for heavy criticism from those who considered the use of nuclear arms to be fundamentally at odds with Christian principles.[26] In a letter to *The*

---

22. J. Hunt to GF, April 3, 1954, GF Papers 142, fol. 371; GF to Hunt, April 5, 1954, GF Papers 142, fol. 372.

23. Kirby, "The Church of England and the Cold War Nuclear Debate." For other letters and papers related to the topic of nuclear weapons and the church's response, see GF Papers 142, fols. 368, 373–408.

24. Fisher to Winchester, April 26, 1954, GF Papers 142, fols. 384–85.

25. *Chronicle of Convocation 1954*, 22–23.

26. Kirby, "The Church of England and the Cold War Nuclear Debate," 282.

Times on January 17, 1956, Bishop Bell opposed these weapons on solid just-war grounds: the same ethical platform from which he had launched his protest against the Allied saturation-bombing campaign in World War II. Hydrogen bombs, he said, "are morally indefensible." They not only "inflict destruction on a colossal scale altogether out of proportion to the end desired"; they also fail to discriminate between military targets and civilian populations. Indeed, the "poison" of their radioactive fallout could end the human race. The bishop of Chichester called upon the American president and the British prime minister "at least to pledge themselves to renounce all further tests, and never to be the first to use hydrogen bombs."[27] The month before Bell's letter appeared, Geoffrey Fisher, in an address to the Royal United Service Institute, had stated his view that the enemy needed to be kept in check by any means necessary: "I believe that every deterrent to Communism—even the Hydrogen Bomb—is good so long as it deters."[28]

But Fisher's developed position on nuclear weapons was more nuanced than this utterance (and similar statements) suggests. His basic ethical stance always was that the value of factual truth—for example, the facts disclosed by scientific discovery—must be examined and weighed in the light of moral truth. In their ethical judgments, Christians must seek out and employ a higher law than that which a purely functional reason points to: just because we can do something—such as build a bigger bomb—does not mean that we ought to. Factual truth should not be considered an end in itself: rather, something is good, Fisher believed, if it can be used for the larger human good. Love, he said, "must condition what uses we make of truth," including the powerful truths of nuclear energy.[29]

As the years went by, then, he too grew more concerned about the ethical justifiability of nuclear weapons, more skeptical of the power of these weapons to prevent conflict, and hence more eager to seek peaceful ways of ending the arms race. To Prime Minster Anthony Eden, Cantuar wrote of "an anxious and growing opinion among the Churches that the British and American Governments must take a fresh initiative *now* in the field of disarmament and atomic warfare if the situation is to be kept under any kind of moral control." In this lengthy letter of January 23, 1956, Fisher told the premier that possessing the hydrogen bomb was justifiable as a deterrent, yes. But all knew that its employment would be

27. Bell, "The Hydrogen Bomb."

28. GF, December 9, 1955, quoted in Kirby, "The Church of England," 279.

29. GF, quoted in Harris, *Conversations*, 71.

suicidal—it "would . . . devastate both sides beyond endurance"—and so use of this tool of war was, in both moral and strategic terms, unthinkable. The "Christian conscience," he said, revolts "against the very existence of such an inhuman and nihilistic weapon." Great Britain, therefore, should work for arms control and reduction, as well as for the prohibition of certain classes of nuclear weapons. By such means both Britain and the United States might "recapture the moral initiative in this field," for the sake of the safety and security of the world.[30]

The Suez Crisis

The foreign-policy debate with which Geoffrey Fisher is most closely identified occurred in the House of Lords during a spirited exchange that he had with the Lord Chancellor, who was attempting to defend the policy of the British government during the Suez Crisis. Fisher's remarks on this occasion were critical of Britain's armed intervention—carried out in collusion with the French and the Israelis—aimed at regaining control of the Suez Canal.

Built by the international Suez Canal Company and opened in 1869, this 106-mile waterway connected the Mediterranean Sea with the Gulf of Suez (and thence with the Red Sea). In 1875 Great Britain became the largest shareholder when Prime Minister Benjamin Disraeli bought 40% of the shares for the government. The Convention of Constantinople, signed in 1888 by all the major European powers, declared the canal neutral and promised free navigation in peace and war. In June 1956, in response to pressure from Egypt, the British completed their evacuation of armed forces from Egypt and the Canal Zone. But in July 1956, after Britain and the United States withdrew their pledges of financial support to help Egypt build the Aswan High Dam, President Gamal Abdal Nasser nationalized the Suez Canal, replacing the privately owned company that had managed the canal with the Egyptian Canal Authority. On October 29, 1956, Israel, which had been denied passage through the canal since 1950, invaded Egyptian territory. Then Britain and France dispatched armed forces to retake the canal.

Fisher's remarks in the House of Lords on Thursday, November 1, 1956, came the day after British attacks had begun. Following Egypt's refusal to comply with an ultimatum to withdraw from the canal, British and French troops moved in, with Canberra bombers swooping down from bases in

30. GF to Anthony Eden [copy], January 23, 1956, National Archives FO 371/123119/ ZE 112/39 1956. Used by permission.

Cyprus. The British government alleged that the invasion was to keep the peace; in fact its aim was to topple President Nasser, who had closed the canal. The day after Fisher's intervention in the Lords, the United Nations General Assembly met in emergency session and approved an American resolution calling for a ceasefire, which Cantuar was in favor of.[31]

Fisher regarded the British action as a violation of his nation's responsibilities under the United Nations Charter.[32] In the House of Lords, he persistently questioned the Lord Chancellor, Lord Kilmuir, trying to induce the government to admit that Britain was an aggressor, not the defensive power. "The point I remember," Fisher later said, "is that Kilmuir made a great speech in defence of Government policy. At some point he asserted that we were only going into Egypt as a fire-engine to extinguish a blaze." Like many other Britons, Fisher had doubts about this characterization of the circumstances. He launched into the Lord Chancellor. "I intervened and asked a question, referring to the fact that the forces of Israel were twenty miles or more inside Egyptian soil. But the Lord Chancellor would not see it, and so I went on trying to make him admit that Great Britain and Israel were both invading Egypt as an act of war. A fierce exchange followed, embalmed now in the pages of *Hansard* [the official record of Parliament]."[33]

Lord Kilmuir asserted that Egypt was the attacking power and refused to acknowledge that Great Britain, France, and Israel together had undertaken this attack. "Embalmed" in *Hansard* are Fisher's pointed comments and questions: "We cannot ignore the fact that the President of the United States thinks that we have made a grave error. We cannot ignore the fact . . . that world opinion on the whole . . . is convinced that we have made a grave error. . . ." Fisher believed that a "strong case" could be made "for saying that our action is a contravention of the United Nations Charter." He acknowledged the existence of "a good argument" for taking the action that Britain took, but he had serious concerns. The British people, he remarked, were "perplexed and alarmed."[34]

Then the archbishop directly challenged the Lord Chancellor, the Right Honourable Viscount Kilmuir. "My Lords, the noble and learned Viscount referred to the attacking Power against which we have to exercise self-defence. Who is the attacking Power?" The Lord Chancellor answered

31. Sandbrook, *Never Had It So Good,* 17; Carpenter, *Archbishop Fisher,* 405.

32. Carpenter, *Archbishop Fisher,* 402.

33. Quoted in Purcell, *Fisher of Lambeth,* 261–62.

34. GF, November 1, 1956, *The Parliamentary Debates (Hansard): House of Lords Official Report* (London: Her Majesty's Stationery Office, 1957) 199:1294, 1295.

that self-defense can mean "the protection of nationals on someone else's territory." He argued that if, after "a peaceful landing," the nation we are invading "says that they will resist with all their force," then we have a right to defend ourselves. "Which is the attacking Power in this case?" Fisher asked. "[T]he person who threatens to use force in answer to a proffered peaceful intervention," Lord Kilmuir replied. "Who is this attacking Power?" Fisher persisted. "Egypt," the Lord Chancellor said. Fisher led Lord Kilmuir to acknowledge that there were actually two stages of attack and defense, the first initiated when Israel invaded Egypt. "You omitted to mention the first," he told the Lord Chancellor. "I have now inserted it."[35]

Lord Jowett, who had been a schoolmate of Geoffrey Fisher's at Marlborough, said to the archbishop on their way out, "Well, Fisher, that's one of the best pieces of cross-examination I've ever heard."[36] But Cantuar later appeared to regret that his cross-questioning of the Lord Chancellor had been as stinging as it was.[37]

Fisher's anti-Suez position was not widely popular; many criticized him for speaking out as he did. But Cantuar continued to insist that the British people were divided on Suez and that their misgivings should be openly acknowledged. Throughout November and December of 1956, Fisher was remarkably well informed, through his own well-placed sources in Downing Street, about what had been happening behind the scenes. Cantuar's involvement was an instance of a key establishment figure not only expressing an opinion in public but also possessing key intelligence to back it up: information, for example, about Britain's confidential negotiations—collusion—prior to the Suez military operation.[38]

The British government, led by Sir Anthony Eden, thought that the American government, led by Dwight D. Eisenhower, would give Britain, France, and Israel its support.[39] But Eden badly misjudged the amount of American and other international backing he would receive. Most of the world viewed the Suez invasion as a serious blunder, an aggressive action wrong in itself and undertaken at precisely the wrong moment in world history. In early November 1956 Soviet tanks rolled into Budapest, Hungary, to put down the popular anti-Communist revolution that had broken out there.

---

35. Ibid., 1352–54.
36. Quoted in Carpenter, *Archbishop Fisher*, 404.
37. Carpenter, *Archbishop Fisher*, 405.
38. Thorpe, *Eden*, 524–25, 540–41.
39. See Tony Judt, *Postwar*, 295.

Certainly the U.S. president had no intention of being pulled into a conflict in the Middle East. He and his secretary of state, John Foster Dulles, were totally against using force to settle the dispute.[40] In fact, what pushed the British out of Egypt was economic pressure from the American government.[41] On December 22 the British and the French completed their withdrawal from Suez, and on January 9, 1957, an ailing and exhausted Sir Anthony announced his resignation as prime minister.[42]

The Coronation of Queen Elizabeth II

Geoffrey Fisher had a high view of the monarchy and hence of the ceremony in which the King or Queen is crowned. He saw the coronation service as far more than a major media event; or, if it was inescapably that, then a media event whereby the message of Christianity—in particular, the message that England was still a Christian state, responsible to God—could be delivered to millions. Writing of the coronation service in 1953, E. C. Ratcliff, the Ely Professor of Divinity at Cambridge University, made exactly this point about the larger meaning of the ceremony: "The Coronation Service . . . reflects the persistent English intertwining of sacred and secular, of civil and ecclesiastical. It reflects particularly the historic English conception of the mutual relations of Sovereign, Church and People, and of all three to God. . . . [It] symbolises national continuity . . . *sub specie Christianitatis*."[43]

Most of all, then, Geoffrey Fisher viewed the coronation service as a quintessentially religious ceremony. He "possessed a fine and eminently audible voice," notes Edward Carpenter, "though he lacked Lang's rare quality of lifting a ceremony into a world of drama and mystery. What he could do was to introduce a straightforward spiritual intention. Supremely

40. Sandbrook, *Never Had It So Good*, 11–12.

41. Ibid., 21.

42. For an overview of the Suez affair in its various aspects—legal and financial, as well as political and military—see Hennessy, *Having It So Good*, 405–57. The strained relationship between GF and Anthony Eden went back at least to December 1955, when Cantuar and the prime minister differed on important ecclesiastical appointments. The chief point of disagreement concerned the translation of Michael Ramsey, the bishop of Durham: Should he go to York (Eden's view) or to London (Fisher's preference)? See Thorpe, *Eden*, 446–47.

43. Ratcliff, *The Coronation Service of Her Majesty Queen Elizabeth II*, 23. "Our Coronation Order expresses in the most vivid way the ideal relationship between Church and State; the archbishop representing the Church, and the king the State. . . ." Garbett, *Church and State in England*, 121.

was this the case with the Coronation."[44] The Queen, Fisher said, is "called by God" and "consecrated by God."[45]

The British sovereign no longer possessed much temporal power, but this fact only increased, in Fisher's view, her spiritual authority. That's part of what he wanted to convey before and during the service. "The executive power, the power to rule and govern, to order and compel, has been steadily taken from our monarchs," Fisher declared. "But this diminution of temporal power has given to the Sovereign the possibility of a spiritual power far more exalted and far more searching in its demands: the power to lead, to inspire, to unite, by the Sovereign's personal character, personal conviction, personal example; by the simplicity of a sincere heart, by the sympathy of a generous soul; by the graces of God."[46]

The young Queen largely shared her archbishop's view of the sacred character of this event. To help prepare her spiritually, Fisher put together for her use *A Little Book of Private Devotions.* A historian of the monarchy has said of Elizabeth: "Both the oath and the anointing were viewed by her as pivotal events in her life, seen as acts of personal dedication to the service of the nation."[47] The anointing was the most solemn and sacred part of the coronation ritual. It took place out of view of both the cameras and the congregation. Divested of royal robes and adornments and wearing a simple white dress, the Queen moved to St. Edward's chair. With the oil of chrism the archbishop anointed her by making a sign of the cross on her palms, on her chest, and on her head, saying: "By thy Head anointed with holy Oil: as kings, priests, and prophets were anointed. And as Solomon was anointed King by Zadok the priest and Nathan the prophet, so be thou anointed, blessed and consecrated Queen over the Peoples, whom the Lord thy God hath given thee to rule and govern. . . ."[48]

Shortly thereafter, the archbishop of Canterbury lifted the royal crown above the head of the seated Queen, held the crown aloft for a few moments, and then dramatically brought it down upon the sovereign's head. After homages to the Queen by prelates and nobles, there was the acclamation, "God Save Queen Elizabeth. Long live Queen Elizabeth, May the Queen live for Ever!"

44. Carpenter, *Cantuar,* 508–9. See Strong, *Coronation,* 472.

45. GF, "Majesty," in *I Here Present Unto You,* 21.

46. Ibid., 22.

47. Strong, *Coronation,* 431.

48. Ibid., 488; Pimlott, *The Queen,* 213.

The coronation of Queen Elizabeth II took place on June 2, 1953. It was the first major royal celebration to be televised. In these early days of the medium, only three million Britons owned television sets, but the ceremony reached an audience estimated at 20 to 27 million people, which was half the adult population. Another 12 million people followed the coronation on the radio.[49] A recent writer in the *Times Literary Supplement* refers to this event as "the most magnificent public spectacle of twentieth-century Britain."[50]

The coronation of Elizabeth II arrived at a propitious moment in the history of the British monarchy. "When George died in 1952," notes a historian of this period, "the Windsors were far more popular than they had been at his accession, and his daughter Elizabeth succeeded to the throne with probably as much public goodwill as any that had gone before her."[51] Rose Macaulay, however, could not resist issuing a demurral: "No doubt all pleased by the coronation service and its ceremonies," she wrote to an English priest in the United States, "though its expense must seem to them wildly excessive, as indeed it does to me, when money is so badly needed for our old and only barely subsisting poor people, and so many other things."[52]

Macaulay's comment adumbrates a time only a few years hence when the fortunes of the monarchy would start to decline, and people would indeed begin to ask if it was worth all the money expended. Being tied together with the church as central parts of "the Establishment" turned out to be a mixed blessing for both venerable institutions. The coronation service, writes A. N. Wilson in *After the Victorians*, "was in part a splendid piece of religio-patriotic pageantry to celebrate great things which deserved celebration: peace, freedom, prosperity." But, he says, this service "can now be seen as a consoling piece of theatre, designed to disguise from themselves the fact that the British had indeed, as Dean Acheson so accurately remarked nearly a decade later, lost an empire and failed to find a

---

49. Sandbrook, *Never Had It So Good*, 41.

50. Saul, "The Pomp of Power," 26. See also Hennessy, *Having It So Good*, 233–49. Hennessy is particularly good on the reaction of the people of Scotland, where nationalist sentiment was strong. When the dean of Westminster, Alan Don, a Scotsman, suggested that the Moderator of the (Presbyterian) Church of Scotland have a role in the Coronation, GF saw the wisdom of this accommodation and readily agreed (247).

51. Sandbrook, *Never Had It So Good*, 41.

52. Rose Macaulay to Rev. Hamilton Johnson, December 5, 1952, in *Last Letters to a Friend, 1952–1958*, 56.

role."[53] By the end of Geoffrey Fisher's tenure of office, the observer might well ask, what was the role of the archbishop of Canterbury, and how well did Fisher fill that role?

53. Wilson, *After the Victorians*, 528.

7

Retirement: 1961–1972

Deciding to Retire

In early 1961, as he approached his seventy-fourth birthday, Geoffrey Fisher decided that it was time to retire. He had held episcopal office for almost thirty years—in an era before bishops took sabbaticals—and his customary ardor for committees and conferences was cooling. He was in good health, but he felt mentally fatigued and his famous energy was starting to flag. Upcoming events that would require Cantuar's participation—the Third Assembly of the World Council of Churches in New Delhi, 1961; the Anglican Congress in Toronto, 1963—he did not look forward to with his usual good humor.[1]

Sometimes when a man or woman reaches a certain age, the personality's internal governor becomes less constraining, more complaisant, in relation to the less-attractive impulses of the self. So it was with Geoffrey Fisher in the last year or two of his archiepiscopate. He talked more and listened less. He became more impatient, more prone to dominate discussions, less willing to hear opposing views. Particularly was this the case at Bishops' Meetings, where he might speak for a full hour without let-up. At such times he must have been all but insufferable to those whom protocol obliged to sit quietly and look attentive. The archbishop's domestic chaplain boldly ventured to tell him he was talking too much. Graciously, Fisher took this message to heart, assessed the situation, and decided to resign. On January 17, 1961, he announced his retirement to the Convocation of Canterbury.[2] When he stepped down on May 31, he was offered a life barony, which he accepted. He and his wife became Lord and Lady Fisher of Lambeth.

1. Carpenter, *Archbishop Fisher*, 748.
2. Ibid., 747; Chadwick, *Michael Ramsey*, 106.

Whom should the prime minister appoint as his successor? Fisher preferred the evangelical Donald Coggan, bishop of Bradford, to the more-obvious choice, Michael Ramsey, archbishop of York. The latter, Cantuar believed, was too much a party man—too closely allied with the Catholic wing of the Church of England—to be either a strong supporter of church reunion efforts or a consistent opponent of Catholic liturgical extremes. As we have already seen, Ramsey did not share Fisher's positive view of canon law as a means of bringing about order in worship.[3] Also, Fisher doubted that Ramsey possessed the requisite managerial skills—or the commitment to administration—to deal effectively with the huge work-load at Lambeth. In Fisher's opinion, Ramsey spent too much time on theology and too little time on administrative business. For these reasons, Fisher did not feel that he could urge Harold Macmillan to recommend to the Queen that Michael Ramsey be translated from York to Canterbury.[4]

But if Fisher supposed that Macmillan shared his view of what was needed in an archbishop of Canterbury, then he badly mistook his man. The prime minister was looking for a spiritual leader first and foremost; he was not unduly bothered by the fact that Ramsey was an indifferent administrator.[5] The church "had had enough of Martha and it was time for some Mary," Macmillan is reported to have commented later, explaining his decision.[6] The premier drew his analogy from the story in Luke's Gospel (10:38–42) which offers the contrast between Martha, busy about her many tasks, and Mary, the type of contemplatives.

Thus Macmillan made up his mind, according to his own lights; the opinion of the outgoing Primate of All England mattered little to him. Michael Ramsey relished telling the story of his conference with the premier concerning the selection of Geoffrey Fisher's successor. Several different accounts of this meeting have been handed down. This one is Owen Chadwick's version: "Macmillan said to Ramsey, 'Fisher doesn't seem to approve of you.' Ramsey defended him. 'Fisher,' he said, 'was my head-master and he has known all my deficiencies for a long time.' 'Well,' said Macmillan, 'he is not going to be my headmaster.'"[7]

3. Chadwick, *Michael Ramsey*, 103; Margaret Pawley, *Donald Coggan*, 126. Fisher also may have questioned Ramsey's commitment to Church Establishment. Michael De-la-Noy, *Michael Ramsey*, 140.

4. Chadwick, *Michael Ramsey*, 104.

5. Ibid., 105.

6. Quoted in Chadwick, *Michael Ramsey*, 107. Chadwick takes this reported statement to be an authentic utterance by Macmillan.

7. Chadwick, *Michael Ramsey*, 107. Cf. De-la-Noy, *Michael Ramsey*, 139; and

Trent

In 1961 Geoffrey and Rosamond Fisher moved to Dorsetshire, a county in southwest England on the English Channel. At first they lived in the small town of Sherborne, but in 1962 they took up residence in a redundant rectory in Trent, a village of 300 people in rural Dorset; and there they remained. Geoffrey Fisher became curate-in-charge of the parish church, taking services on Sundays and calling on parishioners during the week. He followed a standard routine. After breakfast he would go to his study, write letters, and read *The Times*. In mid-morning the rector of the parish was likely to call, and the two men would talk over matters both civil and ecclesiastical. After lunch and a brief rest, Fisher would go for a walk, visiting the people of the village. Soon he knew all of them, not only their names but also their circumstances. If on his walkabout he encountered someone he did not recognize, he would ask him or her, "And who are *you?*" Decades after his own youth, he experienced in Trent something like the community he had known and felt secure in as a boy. He was always good with young people, easy and natural with them. One evening each week he played chess with a boy in the village. With everyone he was approachable and friendly. If he was out walking and thought he would like a cup of tea, he could knock on a cottage door and enjoy it with one of his neighbors.[8] The way that he lived his retirement in Trent gave Geoffrey Fisher's career as an Anglican clergyman a rounded-off quality, as he embraced an opportunity in parish ministry that his early turn to schoolmastering had denied him.

Both Fishers loved the life of this English country village. In 1967 they celebrated their golden wedding anniversary and Geoffrey Fisher's eightieth birthday. In April of that year Queen Elizabeth and Prince Philip entertained them at Windsor Castle, and in May the residents of Trent held a reception in the Fishers' honor in the hall of the local church school.[9] When Geoffrey Fisher died in 1972, he was buried in Trent rather than in Canterbury Cathedral. After her husband's death, Rosamond Fisher lived in the village rectory for another ten years.[10]

Carpenter, *Archbishop Fisher*, 750.

  8. Carpenter, *Archbishop Fisher*, 754, 767, 770.

  9. Ibid., 753.

  10. Ibid., 751.

Anglican-Methodist Reunion

If Geoffrey Fisher had confined himself to the modest life sketched above, then he would have offered to posterity the very model of an archiepiscopal retirement. Observers would have witnessed something new: an active man's graceful withdrawal from high office followed by humble service on behalf of his adopted community. Even for Christian leaders, however, the self is more often a chiaroscuro of light and dark than an unbroken plane of radiant goodness. To the portrait of Geoffrey Fisher, retired, the shadow of pride adds depth, making the subject more interesting, if not more appealing.

Episcopal prerogatives and the habits of authority must be hard to leave behind. In retirement, Fisher still insisted—against standard practice—on being addressed as Your Grace and on being referred to as Archbishop—rather than Bishop—Fisher.[11] Worse, he could not manage to do the right thing and refrain from interfering with the efforts of his successor. No one, including his wife, could prevail upon him to hold back.[12] Fisher did everything he could to torpedo the chances of the Anglican-Methodist reunion scheme. He campaigned against the proposal, wrote letters denouncing it, and published articles and pamphlets criticizing its terms. In July 1969 the Methodist Conference approved the plan, but the Church of England turned it down, declining to affirm the proposal by the necessary majority.[13]

Ironically, Geoffrey Fisher, the Protestant-leaning archbishop who had reached out to the Free Churches in his Cambridge sermon of 1946, opposed the union scheme; while Michael Ramsey, the Anglo-Catholic who Fisher feared might drag his feet on ecumenism, endorsed it. Fisher's excessive involvement in the debate and his public disagreement with his successor embarrassed Michael Ramsey.[14] "The Trent postmark," Ramsey

11. De la Noy, *Michael Ramsey*, 140

12. Carpenter, *Archbishop Fisher*, 756.

13. Ibid., 757. Fisher set forth his objections to the proposal in a pamphlet titled *Covenant and Reconciliation*, published in 1967. Wanting to make certain that the scheme would have sufficient backing in both churches if the measure did pass, the Methodist and the Anglican churches decided that a 75% majority would be necessary for the proposal to be approved. On July 8, 1969, the Methodist Conference approved the reunion scheme with 77% in favor, but that same day the Convocations of Canterbury and York could muster only a 69% majority. The proposal was revived and voted on by the General Synod (established in 1970) in May 1972, when it received less than 66% in favor, and therefore was allowed to lapse.

14. Edwards, *Leaders of the Church of England, 1828–1978*, 366.

would mutter in retirement; "now, the Trent postmark always filled me with a feeling of doom."[15] Apparently Fisher could not stop thinking of himself as Michael's headmaster, providing needed direction to his pupil.[16] Glimpsing the Trent postmark on an envelope containing another piece of unsought counsel, Ramsey sometimes simply dropped the disquieting item into the wastebasket.[17] He stopped answering these epistles, leading Fisher to register a formal complaint with the Standing Committee of the General Synod that he was not being properly treated by Archbishop Ramsey.[18]

In his opposition to Anglican-Methodist amalgamation, Fisher was more consistent than he might at first appear. He had always preferred full communion to union—thereby anticipating the path of successful ecumenism over the next quarter-century. He had never supported a total merger of the Church of England with any Protestant church. What he did favor was a federation of autonomous churches, which—once the Protestant bodies had incorporated episcopacy into their systems—would share ministries and the sacraments but hold on to their distinctive liturgies and historic identities.[19]

Fisher worried that organic union would mean the end not only of the Church of England as the Established Church but also of the Church of England as the center of the Anglican Communion. Consequently, he risked offending many of his natural allies in the church by lending his name and stature to a group of reunion opponents who, without his assistance, might have failed to defeat the union scheme when it came up for a vote in the Convocations.[20]

Death

In 1972 Geoffrey Fisher's health began to decline, and on Thursday, September 14, at age eighty-five, he suffered a stroke. When his wife, Rosamond, came to his side as he lay prostrate, he said to her, "Don't both-

15. De la Noy, *Michael Ramsey*, 200.

16. Chadwick, *Michael Ramsey*, 115.

17. Jonathan Mantle, *Archbishop*, 125.

18. Chadwick, *Michael Ramsey*, 115.

19. Staples, "Archbishop Geoffrey Francis Fisher: An Appraisal," 258. See GF, *Covenant and Reconciliation*, 5–6.

20. Edwards, *Leaders*, 366–67. Edwards observes that a difficulty with Fisher's approach to ecumenism was that while Fisher did not support proposals for union with the Free Churches, none of the Free Churches would have been interested in taking episcopacy into its system unless doing so did result in union with the Church of England.

er me, dear, I'm busy dying." He was taken to the hospital in Sherborne. Fortunate to the end, he had an easy death, dying peacefully in his sleep just one day after being stricken. Five days later, his funeral service was held in the Trent church.[21] In 1982 Lady Fisher moved to Wimbledon to live with a member of her family.[22] She died in 1986 and her body was interred alongside her husband's in a vault beneath the cross in the churchyard at Trent.[23]

Leadership

People used to quote Ralph Waldo Emerson's dictum from "Self-Reliance" (1841) that "[a]n institution is the lengthened shadow of one man." Properly understood, this statement merely reminds us of the large impact, for good or ill, of the person at the top. Misinterpreted, Emerson's saying can gull the unthinking into supposing that the finest leadership is the most unitary and self-reliant; or that the best leader is a dominating figure, seeking to control everything. But as every good administrator knows, these mistaken conclusions overlook the vital yin-yang of leadership. Like the author of Ecclesiastes, the wise leader knows that to everything there is a season: a time to cast a shadow and a time to stand out of the light.

The yang of academic leadership, for example, is accomplishing good by actively working to bring about the best conditions for teaching and learning. The yin of academic leadership is accomplishing good by hiring an excellent staff and then making space for their distinctive contributions. In liberating others, the withholding is as crucial as the giving.

Early in his professional career, as a young headmaster, Geoffrey Fisher must have grasped these basic principles. In fact, one of his biographers notes precisely this point. In his book *A Class of Their Own*, which discusses headmasters who became archbishops of Canterbury, Bernard Palmer points out Fisher's skill in choosing faculty leaders who could effectively manage their own shops. Palmer writes that in Fisher's view, "the key to the successful running of a school curriculum . . . lay in the choice of really good heads of department. He flattered himself that he had been successful in his selection of first-rate men, particularly in the middle period of his headmastership." The result was "a steady flow of university scholarships" and an improvement in the intellectual tenor of

21. Carpenter, *Archbishop Fisher*, 762.

22. Ibid., 763.

23. Ibid.

the institution. Several men who had been staff members under Fisher at Repton went on to preside over their own schools.[24]

Geoffrey Fisher's positive achievements as headmaster—and especially as archbishop—are best understood in terms of both doing and not-doing. Of course, the world being what it is, someone proficient in the Tao of leadership may not receive all the recognition that he or she is entitled to. Charles Smyth recounts the following story about Fisher and his reputation:

> "Mark my words," observed a well-known dignitary of the Church of England, who had been closely associated with the Primate at one stage of his career: "when Geoffrey was Headmaster of Repton, everybody said 'What a good school Repton is,' but nobody ever said 'What a great Headmaster Fisher is!' When he was Bishop of London, everybody said: 'How well the Diocese is running' but nobody said 'How admirably Fisher is running it!' And it will be the same all his life."[25]

Both this statement and the earlier one by Bernard Palmer about choosing capable department heads contain clues to the nature of sound leadership and insights into the biography of Geoffrey Fisher. Together they suggest a way to assess his career, for, unlike both his successor and his predecessor in the Chair of Augustine of Canterbury, Fisher was first and last an administrator. A scholarly bishop may be judged by his wisdom and a prophetic bishop by his courage *contra mundum*, but an administrator-bishop must be judged chiefly by his results.

Fisher's archiepiscopate is most vulnerable to criticism in those areas in which he might have asserted a more imaginative style of leadership or in which he dominated or interfered when he should have let go. He was most successful when, informed by the virtues of prudence and temperance, he handled the yin-yang of leadership like an adept. To cite two major examples, he knew when the time was right to initiate a meeting with the pope, and he was happy to encourage and assist Anglicans in Africa as they formed autonomous provinces. An authority on the history of the development of the Anglican Communion makes a significant observation about this aspect of Fisher's leadership: "his experience as a headmaster probably made him willing to risk delegating responsibility."[26]

24. Bernard Palmer, *A Class of Their Own*, 163.
25. Smyth, "G.F.F.: An Appreciation," in Thomas, *Repton, 1557–1957*, 112.
26. Jacob, *The Making of the Anglican Church Worldwide*, 267–68.

By loosening the bonds, he not only preserved but also strengthened the unity of the Anglican Communion.[27]

Geoffrey Fisher or George Bell?

The most famous appraisal of Fisher's leadership came from the pen of the prominent theologian Donald MacKinnon (1913–94). His comment appeared in a footnote to an article that he published in *Theology* in 1963: "The historians of the Church of England," he said, "may yet recognize that the worst misfortune to befall its leadership in the end of the war was less the premature death of William Temple than his succession by Fisher of London, and not by Bell of Chichester."[28]

Weighty words, but they should be taken with a heavy discount, for D. M. MacKinnon was predisposed to deplore almost everything about Geoffrey Fisher. The Norris-Hulse Professor of Philosophical Theology at Cambridge University, MacKinnon, in the words of Iris Murdoch's biographer, "certainly had instinctively radical social and political principles—the oft-repeated tale of his climbing under the table to bite the calf of a visiting Anglican bishop has only symbolic truth: he was at odds with what would later be termed the Establishment."[29] Frequently iconoclastic, MacKinnon naturally preferred the more-liberal bishop of Chichester, whose "steadfast fidelity in protest against the policy of obliteration bombing" he particularly admired.[30]

Even with a substantial discount, MacKinnon's words carry heft and warrant a response. Every biographer of Fisher or historian of the postwar Church of England has had to ask if MacKinnon was right: Was Bell preferable to Fisher? The question is unavoidable, but the answer is elusive—not only because it relies on guesswork but also because the two men appear to have been roughly equal in their varying qualities. Indeed, although MacKinnon's phrasing of the issue makes it sound as if the truth of the matter is clear and that even church historians would eventually recognize it, both Fisher's strengths and Bell's weaknesses were greater than MacKinnon acknowledged. It is doubtful that Bell would have been significantly better than Fisher in the role of archbishop of Canterbury. But MacKinnon was essentially correct: Bell probably was the wiser choice. The reason why this is so points up the unfairness of the question itself,

27. Smyth, "In Duty's Path," 70.
28. MacKinnon, "Justice," 102n.
29. Conradi, *Iris Murdoch*, 130.
30. MacKinnon, *Themes in Theology*, 124.

however, for the answer must take into account what no one in 1945 could have foreseen: the period of the tumultuous 1960s and beyond.

"In Good Heart"

In sheer statistical terms, the Church of England under Geoffrey Fisher fared reasonably well. Although the number of baptisms continued to drop in the 1950s, the number of confirmations rose steadily until 1960.[31] Taking a long view and putting the data of the various communions into perspective, Adrian Hastings notes that "there had been no very sharp statistical alteration in the religious practice of England between 1890 and 1960: Free Church figures fell fairly considerably, Roman Catholic figures rose, [and] the Anglican decline was pretty steady but seldom appeared calamitous." He points out that "in 1895 there were 641 Anglican baptisms per thousand live births; in 1960, 554. They had first risen and then fallen in the meantime, but not dramatically so." In addition, "over 60 per cent of all marriages were in an Anglican church in the 1890s; they were still almost 50 per cent in 1960." Nor did the number of Easter communicants drop precipitously. "The Newcastle diocese in 1960 had 39,977 Easter communicants—the highest it had ever had; this represented 6.4 per cent of the population over fifteen, just about the same proportion as that of the 21,216 Easter communicants of 1891." The Church of England had experienced a drop in participation in the interwar years, but this decline was "somewhat reassuringly, if really only rather slightly, reversed in the 1950s, so that there was no expectation of the sort of sudden statistical collapse which was . . . to take place [in the 1960s and 1970s]."[32]

In assessing the church's leadership, perhaps the most telling statistic is the number of men going into the Anglican ministry. This measure might provide the best indication of the perceived vitality of the church, for who would want to sign on with the crew of a sinking ship? And, as we have seen, Fisher himself had worked hard to improve the lot of the parish clergy. In 1958 the number of men ordained was 505, the highest number in several years. Two years later, 599 men were ordained. In 1962 there were more men ordained—628—than in any year since before the First World War.[33] In the mid-1960s the numbers started to go down again:

31. Davie, *Religion in Britain since 1945*, 52.

32. Hastings, *A History of English Christianity*, 551. For more statistical data on religious participation in the 1950s and 1960s, see Brown, *The Death of Christian Britain*, chaps. 7–8.

33. *Men for the Ministry*, n.p. ; Sampson, *Anatomy of Britain Today*, 183. See Garbett,

592 in 1965, 436 in 1969, 392 in 1971.[34] By 1976 there were only 273 ordinations.[35]

Any number of cultural factors lie behind these changes, but the robust role played by Geoffrey Fisher should not be entirely overlooked. He conveyed the impression of having the ecclesiastical situation well in hand; where there were problems, he would search them out and tirelessly work to find solutions.[36] He was the type of useful administrator who is often most preferred by those who do the main work of an institution. By the end of Fisher's tenure of office, the late 1950s, the Church of England appeared to be doing well. Trevor Beeson calls this period "an Indian summer for the church." He notes the data that we have also remarked: "The number of Confirmation candidates and, more significantly, the number of ordinations began to rise." He comments that the parish clergy felt these changes and welcomed them. A new breed of quite able clergymen "believed that the Church of England was ripe for a new reformation. . . . An editorial in the *Church of England Newspaper* in 1960 informed its readers that 'A new Church of England is being born, a church efficient, sophisticated and progressive, a church with money enough and to spare.'"[37]

At this point one cannot help recalling the work of Geoffrey Fisher in reorganizing the finances of the Church of England, in particular by establishing a new agency called the Church Commissioners: a practical endeavor that directly affected morale.[38] It is no wonder that Fisher declared, when he was about to retire, that he left the Church of England "in good heart."[39] Grace Davie believes that "there was, in the 1950s at least, a distinct feeling of well-being, of revival even, within church circles."[40]

Church and State in England, 278–79.

34. Beeson, *The Church of England in Crisis*, 46–47.

35. Hastings, *History*, 551–52.

36. See Purcell, *Fisher of Lambeth*, 93, 94.

37. Beeson, *The Church of England in Crisis*, 174.

38. Andrew Chandler, the historian of the Church Commissioners, comments that GF may not have been loved by those who go in for flashy campaigns, but the archbishop's "worth was better known by those who undertook the workaday task of institutional reform." Fisher "perhaps found his element" in his work with the Church Commissioners. The Commissioners themselves "would not see the like of [GF] again, and they would be fortunate to see much at all of those who succeeded him." *The Church of England in the Twentieth Century*, 148.

39. Quoted in Hastings, *History*, 452.

40. Davie, *Religion in Britain since 1945*, 31.

Deficiencies

How well did Geoffrey Fisher prepare the church for what came afterwards? This is the question raised in the introduction. There we heard
the central character in Rose Macaulay's *The Towers of Trebizond*, a young
woman named Laurie, speak of the Church of England as "a great empire
on its way out."[41] In fact, Fisher deserves much credit for his work to
ensure that the church was not on its way out. "None of Fisher's predecessors," correctly notes one commentator on his career, "witnessed the
dismantling of an empire and its conversion into a commonwealth, none
of his predecessors divested himself of responsibility for and oversight of
churches and people in so many parts of the world or on so large a scale."
In addition, "[n]one traveled so far or so often, none worked so long to see
his own church become part of a coming, greater church."[42]

And yet the student of Fisher's life also has a sense of certain deficiencies and missed opportunities in this impressive career. Fisher's reliance
upon rules and traditional structures of authority was excessive. Overly
involved in canon-law reform, he left the church inadequately prepared to
meet the crises of the 1960s. In his episcopal appointments, he typically
played it safe; his undue caution probably cost the church farther down
the road. He generally favored as bishops congenial pastors who would
not challenge his views.[43] "The price of his wholesome disapproval of
slackness or eccentricity in the clergy," an admirer, Charles Smyth, writes,
"was a tendency to favour docile subordinates, a tendency from which the
Church suffered in proportion as the Archbishop's influence on ecclesiastical appointments grew."[44]

Especially during the final years of his archiepiscopate, neither his
standard meeting agenda nor his manner when presiding was open to
much dissent. "During the latter part of his reign," notes Trevor Beeson,
"many of the bishops became frustrated and critical of the amount of time
taken at their meetings by small administrative matters. They also resented
being treated as if they were public school housemasters subject to an increasingly talkative and dictatorial head."[45] A rule-oriented headmaster,
he had a low tolerance for opposition to his authority and for too much

41. Macaulay, *The Towers of Trebizond*, 234.
42. Arblaster, "All the world's a stage. . . .'" 45.
43. Beeson, *The Bishops*, 131.
44. Smyth, "G.F.F.: An Appreciation," in Thomas, *Repton, 1557–1957*, 112.
45. Beeson, *The Bishops*, 131.

questioning of his judgment.[46] "Once he had reached a conclusion himself," writes Eric Kemp, "he saw it almost as moral obliquity in others not to accept that he was right."[47]

A leader who has been called "the last true representative of the old order," Fisher identified himself too closely with the settled arrangement of society.[48] Nowhere was this identification more clearly stated than in the coronation of Queen Elizabeth. This event, Grace Davie writes, "embodied in high-profile form what might be termed the establishment spirit of the 1950s."[49] When this establishmentarian ethos came under attack in the 1960s, Fisher and the church he represented were rendered that much more vulnerable. Even the traditional garb that Fisher wore associated him with what many looked upon as an irrelevant past. "Dressed," David Edwards notes, "in the episcopal costume of apron and gaiters (and rebuking fellow-bishops who preferred trousers), he began to look, while holding office, a figure out of a dead world."[50]

The Established Church was allied not only with the state but also with the higher strata of English society. Trevor Beeson comments: "Whatever the effect of the marriage [of church and state] has been upon the life of the English nation as a whole—good men are divided on the matter—it cannot be denied that the effect upon the Church of England has been to link it permanently with the most privileged sector of English society."[51] When Fisher stepped down in 1961, three-quarters of the bishops had been to public schools, all but three were graduates of Oxford and Cambridge, and two of the others had gone to Trinity College, Dublin.[52]

Cultural historians describe an accelerating pace of change in British society and culture starting in the second half of the 1950s. The popular films of the first half of the decade, such as *Genevieve* (1953) and *Doctor in the House* (1954), have a bright, cheerful tone. After 1955 this upbeat temper gives way to a darker mood of disillusionment and protest. John Osborne's play *Look Back in Anger* is representative. First produced in London in 1956, the year that Suez shattered British confidence and

---

46. Welsby, *A History of the Church of England, 1945–1980*, 10. See Palmer, *A Class of Their Own*, 187.

47. Eric Kemp, "Chairmanly Cantuar," 24.

48. Hastings, *History*, 664.

49. Davie, *Religion in Britain since 1945*, 31.

50. Edwards, *Leaders*, 366.

51. Beeson, *The Church of England in Crisis*, 25.

52. Sampson, *Anatomy of Britain Today*, 180.

illusions of empire, Osborne's play was made into a film in 1958.[53] Fisher's final year as archbishop of Canterbury saw the first publication of a magazine of political and social satire, *Private Eye*, as well as the staging of an irreverent revue, *Beyond the Fringe*, in London's West End. The latter was the work of a group of Cambridge graduates: Alan Bennett, Peter Cook, Dudley Moore, and Jonathan Miller. Large numbers tuned in the following year, 1962, to watch a new program on television: *That Was the Week That Was*, which aided and abetted the spirit of iconoclasm taking hold across the land. None of the venerable institutions of society was safe from ridicule.

While Fisher's episcopal costume may have put the archbishop at increased risk of caricature, a deeper problem for the church was that his style of religion was so readily dismissible, particularly in an age grown intolerant of conventional wisdom and suspicious of traditional practices. In his seminal work *On Religion: Speeches to Its Cultured Despisers* (1799), the German theologian Friedrich Schleiermacher voiced his concerns about the dangers inherent in a religion that has lost its animating spirit. The church is then reduced to relying on its forms and creeds, while the experience that gave rise to them is lost sight of. In the event, the empirical church fails to be the true church. It will have, Schleiermacher said, "a school-mastering, mechanical nature, which indicates that [its members] merely seek to import religion from without."[54] The actual church may also fail to be the true church when it accepts "special privileges" for itself and becomes intimately connected with the interests of the state.[55]

Too often in his administrative manner and almost always in his language Geoffrey Fisher gives the impression of someone who has retained the form but lost touch with the initial impulse—what Schleiermacher called the "sense and taste for the Infinite"—which inspired the form.[56] This impulse, Schleiermacher said, "appears as a surrender, a submission to be moved by the Whole that stands over against man."[57]

When we do witness an expression of this heart of true piety, such as when Fisher is literally moved in Jerusalem, it is a striking event, altogether exceptional. Evidence exists in Fisher's life-story that he saw himself as a

53. Judt, *Postwar*, 300. John Osborne wrote in a widely remarked essay: "My objection to the Royalty symbol is that it is dead; it is the gold filling in a mouthful of decay." John Osborne, in Maschler, *Declaration*, 58.

54. Schleiermacher, *On Religion*, 161.

55. Ibid., 167.

56. Ibid., 39.

57. Ibid., 37.

disciple of Jesus. Trying to determine what to do about the offer of the London bishopric, he agonizes before finally deciding, during holy week, to say yes to the question, "Lovest thou me?" Along the Via Dolorosa, he experiences himself as a participant in the life of Jesus and in the lives of those who make up the Body of Christ.[58] But this vibrant awareness does not come through in his desiccated, mechanical prose. Geoffrey Fisher, said one of his chaplains, F. C. Synge, was "a lover of smoothly running diocesan machinery. Law, rather than Gospel, was the stuff of his sermons."[59] Undoubtedly Fisher meant for us to take his entire life as a witness to his deepest convictions: reorganizing church finances is as holy a work as any other. But the "school-mastering, mechanical nature" of his religion—and of aspects of his leadership—could not have commended itself to many who came after him.

Another way of stating this concern is to ask whether Geoffrey Fisher had sufficient imagination for the challenges he faced. Clearly in a number of areas he did. But perhaps, as Peter Kirk writes, he (or someone else) could have done more "to capture the public imagination for the Church." Writing in 1958, Kirk acknowledges that, in an increasingly secular age, getting across to people "the eternal Christian verities" is not easy. When Fisher speaks, what he says "is often very sensible." But "when Temple pronounced on these things, he somehow made them seem not only right but inevitable; Dr. Fisher, for some strange reason, lacks this touch."[60] The view of Bishop E. W. Barnes may be jaundiced but it is nevertheless of interest. To the author of *The Rise of Christianity*, Fisher also seemed to lack the ability to impart the essence of the Christian faith in a compelling manner. His son, John Barnes, sums up his father's perception by recalling that, to the bishop, "Fisher never seemed quite as real as his three predecessors." He may "have appeared to be more like a puppet operated by red tape."[61]

George Bell had many faults, but he had more imagination than Fisher, and for this reason—as well as for his other virtues, especially the courage he demonstrated in wartime—he might have made a better archbishop of Canterbury.[62] Bell was more drawn to the works of the imagina-

58. Carpenter, *Archbishop Fisher*, 772.

59. Quoted in Purcell, *Fisher of Lambeth*, 88. Synge was his domestic chaplain when Fisher was bishop of London.

60. Kirk, *One Army Strong?*, 72–73. See Staples, "Archbishop Geoffrey Francis Fisher," 253.

61. Barnes, *Ahead of His Age*, 420.

62. Staples, "Archbishop Geoffrey Francis Fisher," 240.

tion, to the presence of the holy in art, drama, and literature.[63] Thus he might have found ways to speak to those unmoved by the rituals and structures of the Established Church.[64]

When Fisher retired, he was succeeded by someone who was indeed a Mary to his Martha: a person renowned, then and since, for his deep spirituality. We can admire Michael Ramsey at the same time that we can appreciate the distinctive achievements of Geoffrey Fisher. We heard F. C. Synge describe Fisher as a "lover of smoothly functioning diocesan machinery," whose sermons contained more law than gospel. We should note that in this same quotation Synge goes on to speak of Fisher as "a very English Anglican, full of common sense and wisdom and kindness and prudence and shrewdness."[65] Those nouns are well chosen and help to round out a review of Fisher's strengths and weaknesses. In an era that included the theologians Austin Farrer and Eric Mascall, the poets T. S. Eliot and John Betjeman, the writers Dorothy L. Sayers and C. S. Lewis, the philosophers Ian Ramsey and Donald MacKinnon, the novelists Barbara Pym and Rose Macaulay, and many other Anglicans of significant accomplishment, Geoffrey Fisher's contribution was both notable and usefully complementary.

63. See Loades, "The Vitality of Tradition," 28–29.

64. See Brown, *God and Enchantment of Place,* 2, 407–8.

65. Quoted in Purcell, *Fisher of Lambeth,* 88.

Bibliography

Primary Sources

Manuscripts

Lambeth Palace Library, London
    Fulham Papers: Fisher
    Fisher Papers
    Lang Papers

National Archives, Kew
    Atomic Energy (FO 371/123119)

Printed sources

Abbott, Walter M., editor. *The Documents of Vatican II*. Piscataway, NJ: New Century, 1966.

Barnes, Ernest William. *The Rise of Christianity*. London: Longmans, Green, 1947.

Bell, George. *The Church and Humanity*. New York: Longmans, Green, 1946.

———. "The Hydrogen Bomb [letter]." *The Times*, January 17, 1956.

The Canons of the Church of England: Canons Ecclesiastical Promulgated by the Convocations of Canterbury and York in 1964 and 1969. London: SPCK, 1969.

The Chronicle of Convocation: Being a Record of the Proceedings of the Convocation of Canterbury. London: SPCK, n.d.

Dahl, Roald. *Boy: Tales of Childhood*. New York: Farrar, Straus & Giroux, 1984.

Dawley, Powel Mills, editor. *Report of the Anglican Congress, 1954*. London: SPCK, 1955.

Fisher, Geoffrey. *I Here Present Unto You: Addresses Interpreting the Coronation of Her Majesty Queen Elizabeth II, Given on Various Occasions by His Grace the Lord Archbishop of Canterbury, Primate of All England*. London: SPCK, 1953.

———. "A Remarkable Campaign." In Charles T. Cook, *London Hears Billy Graham: The Greater London Crusade*, vii–ix. London: Marshall, Morgan & Scott, 1954.

———. *The Archbishop Speaks: Addresses and Speeches by the Archbishop of Canterbury the Most Reverend Geoffrey Francis Fisher*. Edited by Edward Carpenter. London: Evans Brothers, 1958.

———. "Church and Nation." In *The Church and the Nation: Six Studies in the Anglican Tradition*, edited by Charles Smyth, 13–17. London: Hodder & Stoughton, 1962.

———. *Standards of Morality: Christian and Humanist.* London: Mowbray, 1967.

———. *Covenant and Reconciliation: A Critical Examination of the First Report of the English Standing Conference on "Covenanting for Union" and of the Interim Statement of the Anglican-Methodist Unity Commission Entitled "Towards Reconciliation."* London: Mowbray, 1967.

———. *Touching on Christian Truth: The Kingdom of God, the Christian Church and the World.* London: Mowbray, 1971.

———. "A Step Forward in Church Relations." In *The Church of England, 1815–1948: A Documentary History*, edited by R. P. Flindall, 434–41. London: SPCK, 1972.

Flindall, R. P., editor. *The Church of England, 1815–1948: A Documentary History.* London: SPCK, 1972.

Gollancz, Victor. *More for Timothy: Being the Second Installment of an Autobiographical Letter to His Grandson.* London: n.p., 1953.

Gollancz, Victor, and David Somervell. *Political Education at a Public School.* London: Collins, 1918.

———. *The School and the World.* London: Chapman & Hall, 1919.

Harris, Kenneth. "Dr. Geoffrey Fisher, 1959 [interview]." In *Conversations*, 70–87. London: Hodder & Stoughton, 1967.

Kemp, Eric W. *Shy But Not Retiring: The Memoirs of the Right Reverend Eric Waldram Kemp*, edited by Jeremy Matthew Haselock. London: Continuum, 2006.

Lambeth Conference 1948. London: SPCK, 1948.

Lambeth Conference 1958. London: SPCK, 1958.

Macaulay, Rose. *Last Letters to a Friend, 1952–1958*, edited by Constance Babington-Smith. London: Collins, 1962.

———. *Letters to a Friend, 1950–1952*, edited by Constance Babington-Smith. New York: Atheneum, 1962.

———. *The World My Wilderness.* 1950. Reprint, London: Virago, 1983.

———. *The Towers of Trebizond.* 1956. Reprint, New York: New York Review Books, 2003.

Macmillan, Harold. *The Macmillan Diaries: The Cabinet Years, 1950–1957.* Edited by Peter Catterall. London: Macmillan, 2003.

Matthews, W. R. *Memories and Meanings.* London: Hodder & Stoughton, 1969.

Men for the Ministry, 1963. London: Church Information Board for the Central Advisory Council of Training for the Ministry, n.d. [One in a series of annuals; these booklets are available in LPL.]

The Parliamentary Debates (Hansard): House of Lords Official Report.

Ratcliff, Edward C. *The Coronation Service of Her Majesty Queen Elizabeth II.* London: SPCK; Cambridge: Cambridge University Press, 1953.

Report of the Anglican-Methodist Union Commission. London: SPCK, 1968.

Robinson, John A. T. *Christian Freedom in a Permissive Society.* London: SCM, 1970.

Sherrill, Henry Knox. *Among Friends.* Boston: Little, Brown, 1962.

———. "Friends and Bishops." *The Living Church*, September 14, 1952, 7.

Temple, William. Foreword to *Standing Orders of the Church of England: An Attempt to State What Canon Law Is Now in Force*, edited by J.V. Bullard. London: Faith Press, 1934.

Secondary Sources

Adair, John. *The Becoming Church*. London: SPCK, 1977.

Arblaster, Ted. "'All the world's a stage . . .'" *St. Mark's Review* 152 (Summer 1993) 45–46.

Ball, Harold A. "Archbishop Departs from Halifax as Newsmen Enjoy Last Visit." *The Living Church,* October 20, 1946, 6.

Barnes, John. *Ahead of His Age: Bishop Barnes of Birmingham*. London: Collins, 1979.

Barry, F. R. *Mervyn Haigh*. London: SPCK, 1964.

Beeson, Trevor. *The Church of England in Crisis*. London: Davis-Poynter, 1973.

———. *The Bishops*. London: SCM, 2002.

Blackstone, William. *Commentaries on the Laws of England.* 1765. Reprinted, New York: Oceana, 1966.

Booty, John. *An American Apostle: The Life of Stephen Fielding Bayne Jr.* Valley Forge, PA: Trinity, 1997.

Brown, Callum G. *The Death of Christian Britain: Understanding Secularisation, 1800–2000*. New York: Routledge, 2001.

———. *Religion and Society in Twentieth-Century Britain*. Harlow, U.K.: Pearson, 2006.

Brown, David. *God and Enchantment of Place: Reclaiming Human Experience*. Oxford: Oxford University Press, 2004.

Brown, William Francis. "Cardinal Hinsley." In *Through Windows of Memory*, 96–101. London: Sands, 1946.

Bullard, J. V., editor. *Standing Orders of the Church of England: An Attempt to State What Canon Law Is Now in Force*. London: Faith, 1934.

Butler, R. A. *The Art of the Possible*. London: Hamilton, 1971.

Carpenter, Edward. *Cantuar: The Archbishops in Their Office*. London: Cassell, 1971.

———. *Archbishop Fisher: His Life and Times*. Norwich: Canterbury, 1991.

Carpenter, S. C. *Winnington-Ingram: The Biography of Arthur Foley Winnington-Ingram: Bishop of London, 1901–1939*. London: Hodder & Stoughton, 1949.

Chadwick, Owen. *Michael Ramsey: A Life*. Oxford: Clarendon, 1990.

Chandler, Andrew. "Faith in the Nation? The Church of England in the 20th Century." *History Today* 47 (May 1997) 9–15.

———. *The Church of England in the Twentieth Century: The Church Commissioners and the Politics of Reform, 1948–1998*. Woodbridge, U.K.: Boydell, 2006.

Clements, Keith W. *Lovers of Discord: Twentieth-Century Theological Controversies in England*. London: SPCK, 1988.

Conradi, Peter J. *Iris Murdoch: A Life*. New York: Norton, 2001.

Cornwall, Peter. *The Church and the Nation: The Case for Disestablishment*. London: Blackwell, 1983.

Cox, Jeffrey. *The English Churches in a Secular Society: Lambeth 1870–1930*. New York, 1982.

Davie, Grace. *Religion in Britain since 1945: Believing without Belonging*. Oxford: Blackwell, 1994.

Davies, Christie. *Permissive Britain: Social Change in the Sixties and Seventies*. London: Pitman, 1975.

———. "Religion, Politics, and 'Permissive' Legislation." In *Religion, State, and Society in Modern Britain*, edited by Paul Badham, 319–40. Texts and Studies in Religion 43. Lewiston, NY: Mellen, 1989.

———. "The British State and the Power of Life and Death." In *The Boundaries of the State in Modern Britain,* edited by S. J. D. Green and R. C. Whiting, 341–74. Cambridge: Cambridge University Press, 1996.

———. *The Strange Death of Moral Britain.* New Brunswick, NJ: Transaction, 2004.

De-la-Noy, Michael. *Michael Ramsey: A Portrait.* London: Collins, 1990.

———. *The Church of England: A Portrait.* London: Simon & Schuster, 1993.

———. *Mervyn Stockwood: A Lonely Life.* London: Hodder & Stoughton, 1996.

Driver, Christopher. *The Disarmers: A Study in Protest.* London: Hodder & Stoughton, 1964.

Dudley-Smith, Timothy. *John Stott: The Making of a Leader.* Downers Grove, IL: InterVarsity, 1999.

Edwards, David L. *Leaders of the Church of England, 1828–1978.* London: Hodder & Stoughton, 1978.

Edwards, Jill. "The President, the Archbishop and the Envoy: Religion and Diplomacy in the Cold War." *Diplomacy and Statecraft* 6 (1995) 490–511.

Edwards, Ruth Dudley. *Victor Gollancz: A Biography.* London: Gollancz, 1987.

Elmer, Paul. "Anglican Morality." In *The Study of Anglicanism,* edited by Stephen Sykes and John Booty, 325–38. London: SPCK; Philadelphia: Fortress, 1988.

Garbett, Cyril. *The Claims of the Church of England.* London: Hodder & Stoughton, 1947.

———. *Church and State in England.* London: Hodder & Stoughton, 1950.

———. *The Church of England Today.* London: Hodder & Stoughton, 1953.

Green, S. J. D. "The Revenge of the Periphery? Conservative Religion and the Dilemma of Liberal Society in Contemporary Britain." In *Modernity and Religion,* edited by Ralph McInerny, 89–115. Notre Dame: University of Notre Dame Press, 1994.

Grimley, Matthew. *Citizenship, Community, and the Church of England: Liberal Anglican Theories of the State between the Wars.* Oxford: Clarendon, 2004.

Gronn, Peter C. "An Experiment in Political Education: 'V. G.,' 'Slimy,' and the Repton Sixth, 1916–1918." *History of Education* 19 (1990) 1–21.

Habgood, John. *Church and Nation in a Secular Age.* London: Darton, Longman and Todd, 1983.

Hart, A. Tindall. *The Country Priest in English History.* London: Phoenix House, 1959.

Hastings, Adrian. *A History of English Christianity, 1920–2000.* London: SCM, 2001.

Heenan, John C. *Cardinal Hinsley.* London: Burns, Oates & Washbourne, 1944.

Hein, David. "George Bell, Bishop of Chichester, on the Morality of War." *Anglican and Episcopal History* 58 (1989) 498–509.

———. "The Episcopal Church and the Ecumenical Movement, 1937–1997: Presbyterians, Lutherans, and the Future." *Anglican and Episcopal History* 66 (1997) 4–29.

———. *Noble Powell and the Episcopal Establishment in the Twentieth Century.* Studies in Anglican History. Urbana: University of Illinois Press, 2001.

———. "Faith and Doubt in Rose Macaulay's *The Towers of Trebizond.*" *Anglican Theological Review* 88 (2006) 47–68.

Hein, David, and Gardiner H. Shattuck Jr. *The Episcopalians.* Denominations in America. Westport, CT: Praeger, 2004.

Hein, David, and Edward Hugh Henderson, editors. *Captured by the Crucified: The Practical Theology of Austin Farrer.* London: T. & T. Clark / Continuum, 2004.

Hempton, David. "Established Churches and the Growth of Religious Pluralism: A Case Study of Christianisation and Secularisation in England since 1970." In *The Decline of Christendom in Western Europe, 1750–2000*, edited by Hugh McLeod and Werner Ustorf, 81–98. Cambridge: Cambridge University Press, 2003.

Hennessy, Peter. *Never Again: Britain, 1945–1951*. New York: Pantheon, 1994.

———. *Having It So Good: Britain in the Fifties*. London: Allen Lane/Penguin, 2006.

Herklots, H. G. G. *Frontiers of the Church: The Making of the Anglican Communion*. London: Benn, 1961.

Hinchcliff, Peter. "Church-State Relations." In *The Study of Anglicanism*, edited by Stephen Sykes and John Booty, 351–63. London: SPCK; Philadelphia: Fortress, 1988.

Holtby, Robert T. *Robert Wright Stopford, 1901–1976*. London: The National Society for Promoting Religious Education, 1988.

Iremonger, F. A. *William Temple, Archbishop of Canterbury: His Life and Letters*. London: Oxford University Press, 1948.

Jacob, W. M. *The Making of the Anglican Church Worldwide*. London: SPCK, 1997.

Jacobson, Dan. "'If England Was What England Seems': Safety in Spelling Things Out: The Changes of the Last Fifty Years." *Times Literary Supplement*, March 11, 2005, 11.

James, E. O. *A History of Christianity in England*. London: Hutchinson's University Library, 1949.

James, Eric. *A Life of Bishop John A. T. Robinson: Scholar, Pastor, Prophet*. Grand Rapids: Eerdmans, 1988.

Jasper, Ronald C. D. *George Bell: Bishop of Chichester*. London: Oxford University Press, 1967.

Jefferys, Kevin. *Retreat from New Jerusalem: British Politics, 1951–64*. New York: St. Martin's, 1997.

Judt, Tony. *Postwar: A History of Europe since 1945*. New York: Penguin, 2005.

Kemp, Eric W. *The Life and Letters of Kenneth Escott Kirk: Bishop of Oxford, 1937–1954*. London: Hodder & Stoughton, 1959.

———. "Chairmanly Cantuar." *Times Literary Supplement*, April 10, 1992, 23–24.

Kent, John. *William Temple: Church, State, and Society in Britain, 1880–1950*. Cambridge: Cambridge University Press, 1993.

Kirby, Dianne. "The Church of England and the Cold War Nuclear Debate." *Twentieth Century British History* 4 (1993) 250–83.

———. "Responses within the Anglican Church to Nuclear Weapons, 1945–1961." *Journal of Church and State* 37 (1995) 599–622.

———, editor. *Religion and the Cold War*. New York: Palgrave Macmillan, 2003.

Kirk, Peter. *One Army Strong?* London: Faith, 1958.

Leslie, Paul. *A Church by Daylight: A Reappraisement of the Church of England and Its Future*. London: Geoffrey Chapman, 1973.

Loades, Ann. "The Vitality of Tradition: Austin Farrer and Friends." In *Captured by the Crucified: The Practical Theology of Austin Farrer*, edited by David Hein and Edward Hugh Henderson, 15–46. New York and London: T. & T. Clark / Continuum, 2004.

"Lord Fisher of Lambeth: Former Archbishop of Canterbury [Obituary]." *The Times*, September 16, 1972.

Lloyd, Roger. *The Church of England, 1900–1965*. London: SCM, 1966.

Machin, G. I. T. *Churches and Social Issues in Twentieth-Century Britain*. Oxford: Clarendon, 1998.

MacKinnon, Donald M. "Justice." *Theology* 66 (1963) 97–104.

———. *Themes in Theology: The Three-Fold Cord*. Edinburgh: T. & T. Clark, 1987.

Mantle, Jonathan. *Archbishop: The Life and Times of Robert Runcie*. London: Sinclair-Stevenson, 1991.

Maschler, Tom, editor. *Declaration*. New York: Dutton, 1958.

McLeod, Hugh. *Religion and Society in England, 1850–1914*. Basingstoke: Macmillan, 1996.

Mews, Stuart. "The Sword of the Spirit: A Catholic Cultural Crusade of 1940." In *The Church and War*, edited by W. J. Sheils, 409–30. Studies in Church History 20. Oxford: Blackwell, 1983.

Moore, Charles, A. N. Wilson, and Gavin Stamp. *The Church in Crisis*. London: Hodder & Stoughton, 1986.

Moorman, John R. H. *A History of the Church in England*. 3d ed. Harrisburg, PA: Morehouse, 1994.

Murray, Geoffrey. "He Is the Great Reconciler." *News Chronicle*, January 21, 1958, 4–5.

Neill, Stephen. *The Christian Society*. London: Nisbet, 1952.

Nichols, Peter. *The Politics of the Vatican*. New York: Praeger, 1968.

Norman, Edward R. *Church and Society in England, 1770–1970: A Historical Study*. Oxford: Clarendon, 1976.

———. *Christianity and the World Order*. Oxford: Oxford University Press, 1979.

———. "Church and State since 1800." In *A History of Religion in Britain: Practice and Belief from Pre-Roman Times to the Present*, edited by Sheridan Gilley and W. J. Sheils, 277–91. Oxford: Blackwell, 1994.

Page, Robert J. *New Directions in Anglican Theology: A Survey from Temple to Robinson*. New York: Seabury, 1965.

Palmer, Bernard. *High and Mitred: A Study of Prime Ministers as Bishop-Makers, 1837–1977*. London: SPCK, 1992.

———. *A Class of Their Own: Six Public School Headmasters Who Became Archbishop of Canterbury*. Lewes: Book Guild, 1997.

Pattinson, Derek. "Archbishop Fisher: His Life and Times." *Theology* 95 (1992) 388–90.

Paul, Leslie. *A Church by Daylight: A Reappraisement of the Church of England and Its Future*. London: Chapman, 1973.

Pawley, Margaret. *Donald Coggan: Servant of Christ*. London: SPCK, 1987.

Peart-Binns, John S. *Ambrose Reeves*. London: Gollancz, 1973.

———. *Wand of London*. London: Mowbray, 1987.

Pimlott, Ben. *The Queen: A Biography of Elizabeth II*. London: HarperCollins, 1996.

Potter, Harry. *Hanging in Judgment: Religion and the Death Penalty in England from the Bloody Code to Abolition*. London: SCM, 1993.

Prochaska, Frank. *Royal Bounty: The Making of a Welfare Monarchy*. New Haven: Yale University Press, 1995.

Purcell, William. *Fisher of Lambeth: A Portrait from Life*. London: Hodder & Stoughton, 1969.

Raven, C. E. "E.W.B.—The Man for the Moment." *The Modern Churchman* 45 (1955) 11–24.

Reid, Duncan. Review of *Beyond Colonial Anglicanism: The Anglican Communion in the Twenty-first Century*, edited by Ian T. Douglas and Kwok Pui-lan. *Journal of Anglican Studies* 3 (2005) 126–27.

Richards, Jeffrey. "The Coronation of Queen Elizabeth II and Film." *Court Historian* 9 (2004) 67–79.

Robinson, John A. T. *Christian Freedom in a Permissive Society*. London: SCM, 1970.

Rodd, Cyril S. "A Great and Godly Man [Geoffrey Francis Fisher]." *Expository Times* 103 (1992) 288.

Sachs, William L. *The Transformation of Anglicanism: From State Church to Global Communion.* Cambridge: Cambridge University Press, 1993.

Sampson, Anthony. *Anatomy of Britain Today.* New York: Harper & Row, 1965.

Sandbrook, Dominic. *Never Had It So Good: A History of Britain from Suez to the Beatles.* London: Little, Brown, 2005.

Saul, Nigel. "The Pomp of Power." *Times Literary Supplement,* November 25, 2005, 26.

Schleiermacher, Friedrich. *On Religion: Speeches to Its Cultured Despisers.* Translated by John Oman. New York: Harper & Row, 1958.

Sisson, C. H. *Is There a Church of England?* Manchester: Carcanet, 1993.

Smyth, Charles. *Cyril Forster Garbett.* London: Hodder & Stoughton, 1959.

———. *The Church and the Nation: Six Studies in the Anglican Tradition.* London: Hodder & Stoughton, 1962.

———. "In Duty's Path: Fisher of Lambeth." *Theology* 73 (1970) 64–73.

Snape, Henry Currie. "A Dean and an Archbishop." *Modern Churchman,* n.s., 14 (1971) 286–90.

Spinks, G. Stephens. "World War II and Aftermath." In *Religion in Britain since 1900,* edited by G. Stephens Spinks, 215–30. London: Dakers, 1952.

Staples, Peter. "Archbishop Geoffrey Francis Fisher: An Appraisal." *Nederlands Theologisch Tijdschrift* 28 (1974) 239–63.

Strong, Roy. *Coronation: A History of Kingship and the British Monarchy.* London: HarperCollins, 2005.

Sykes, Stephen. *The Integrity of Anglicanism.* London: Mowbray, 1977.

———. "The Genius of Anglicanism." In *The English Religious Tradition and the Genius of Anglicanism,* edited by Geoffrey Rowell, 227–41. Wantage: Ikon, 1992.

Taylor, Vincent. "Living Issues in Biblical Scholarship: The Church and the Ministry." *Expository Times* 62 (1951) 269–74.

Thomas, Bernard, editor. *Repton, 1557–1957.* London: Batsford, 1957.

Thompson, David M. "Theological and Sociological Approaches to the Motivation of the Ecumenical Movement." In *Religious Motivation: Biographical and Sociological Problems for the Church Historian,* edited by Derek Baker, 467–79. Studies in Church History 15. Oxford: Blackwell, 1978.

Thompson, Kenneth A. *Bureaucracy and Church Reform: The Organizational Response of the Church of England to Social Change, 1800–1965.* Oxford: Clarendon, 1970.

Thorpe, D. R. *Eden: The Life and Times of Anthony Eden, First Earl of Avon, 1897–1977.* London: Chatto & Windus, 2003.

Treglown, Jeremy. *Roald Dahl: A Biography.* New York: Farrar, Straus & Giroux, 1994.

Waller, Maureen. *London 1945: Life in the Debris of War.* New York: St. Martin's, 2004.

Walsh, Michael J. "Ecumenism in War-Time Britain: The Sword of the Spirit and Religion and Life, 1940–1945 (1)." *Heythrop Journal* 23 (1982) 243–58.

———. "Ecumenism in War-Time Britain: The Sword of the Spirit and Religion and Life, 1940–1945 (2)." *Heythrop Journal* 23 (1982) 377–94.

Wand, J. W. C. *Anglicanism in History and Today.* New York: Nelson, 1962.

Warren, Heather A. *Theologians of a New World Order: Reinhold Niebuhr and the Christian Realists, 1920–1948.* New York: Oxford University Press, 1997.

Webster, Harvey Curtis. *After the Trauma: Representative British Novelists since 1920.* Lexington: University Press of Kentucky, 1970.

Wedderspoon, Alexander. *Grow or Die: Essays on Church Growth to Mark the 900ᵗʰ Anniversary of Winchester Cathedral*. London: SPCK, 1981.

Weight, Richard. *Patriots: National Identity in Britain, 1940–2000*. London: Macmillan, 2002.

Welsby, Paul A. *A History of the Church of England, 1945–1980*. Oxford: Oxford University Press, 1986.

White, Gavin. "'No-one is Free from Parliament': The Worship and Doctrine Measure in Parliament, 1974." In *Religion and National Identity*, edited by Stuart Mews, 557–65. Studies in Church History 18. Oxford: Blackwell, 1982.

White-Thomson, Ian H. "Fisher, Geoffrey Francis, Baron Fisher of Lambeth." In *DNB, 1971–1980*, 316–18. Oxford: Oxford University Press, 1986.

Williams, A. T. P. "Religion." In *The Character of England*, edited by Ernest Barker, 56–84. Oxford: Clarendon, 1947.

Wilson, A. N. *After the Victorians: The Decline of Britain in the World*. New York: Farrar, Straus & Giroux, 2005.

Wolffe, John. *God and Greater Britain: Religion and National Life in Britain and Ireland, 1843–1945*. London: Routledge, 1994.

Yates, Nigel. *Anglican Ritualism in Victorian Britain, 1830–1910*. Oxford: Oxford University Press, 1999.